Chihuahua

A University of Arizona Southwest Center Book · Joseph C. Wilder, Series Editor

Chihuahua

pictures from the edge

PHOTOGRAPHS BY VIRGIL HANCOCK | ESSAY BY CHARLES BOWDEN

Published in cooperation with the University of Arizona Southwest Center · University of New Mexico Press Albuquerque

© 1996 by the University of New Mexico Press   All rights reserved.   First edition   Library of Congress Cataloging-in-Publication Data
Hancock, Virgil, 1953–   .   Chihuahua : pictures from the edge / photographs by Virgil Hancock; essay by Charles Bowden.—1st ed.   p. cm.
"A University of Arizona Southwest Center Book."   ISBN 0-8263-1739-1 (pbk.)   1. Chihuahua (Mexico : State)—Pictorial works.
2. Mexican-American Border Region—Description and travel.   I. Bowden, Charles.   II Title.   F1261.H38 1996   972'.16'00222—dc20   96-10008   CIP

for my son, wife, and parents

V. H.

for those who walk the line and over it

C. B.

Contents

My experience of Chihuahua, Mexico, was essentially a discovery of the community use and public power of color. Today, in cityscapes across Chihuahua, bright colors constitute a potent presence and force. They coat the walls of grocery stores, mechanic shops, and storefronts of all kinds. They decorate the metal cages standing guard over graves in the cemeteries. Intense rainbows of color light up graffiti in the cities and illuminate the exterior walls of private homes. Vibrant palettes breath life into images of the Virgin of Guadalupe painted on rural roadsides and into giant murals found in downtown streets. In the daily life of Chihuahuans, paint plays many expressive roles. It celebrates: "Los Barateros" explodes in yellow above the street on which shimmers the watery reflection of tires. It warns: Painted on a garage door, a pistol firmly gripped by a flinty, lethal figure topped by a cowboy hat sends an unmistakable message to potential intruders.

Colors in Chihuahua are also transitory. In the course of my many trips to the region, I frequently revisited cities, streets, and buildings only to find them repainted. The cover of this book provides a vivid example. This political mural, "Brigada por la Paz," survived only a few months before it was painted over in a dull tan. Why the mural was covered depends on who was offended. In one story a multinational corporation was affronted. In another a local political party ordered the new coat of paint. I would not be surprised if, at this moment, something else is forming—in color—in its place.

This book—both my photographs and Charles Bowden's text—is visual. I took the photographs with an 8 x 10 wood field camera, using Fuji Velvia film. The focal lengths of the three lenses I employed were 250 mm, 355 mm, and 480 mm. In his essay, Bowden explores the United States–Mexico border region, a new world more cutting-edge than any existing at a distance on either side of the international line. His word pictures create the historical and contemporary context for my photo-

Preface

graphs. The essay and photographs were completed during what can now be seen as the edge of an epoch, the years of the Salinas regime between early 1990 and before the August 1994 presidential elections and the subsequent devaluation of the peso. The images document a period of rising hopes not yet dashed by the gathering economic crisis.

I want to acknowledge the following people for their help at the many stages of this book project. Charles Bowden was a great traveling companion, stimulating conversationalist, and visionary contributor to the book. Joseph Wilder of the University of Arizona Southwest Center was a good friend and an outstanding navigator from the beginning to the completion of the project. Steve Vollmer of the El Paso Museum of Art helped teach me about how to see my own photographic work and made its public exhibition a reality. The staff of the University of New Mexico Press was wonderful, especially my editor, Durwood Ball, whose guidance and support brought this book into being; Kristina Kachele who designed and produced a book unerringly sympathetic to the text and photographs; and Dana Asbury whose early editorial encouragement was very important and whose help in the preparation of the book was critical.

Most of all I want thank my wife Judith who put up with all my trips to Mexico and was loving and supportive throughout.

Virgil Hancock
Tucson, Arizona
7 May 1996

corrida in black velvet

Charles Bowden

Ojos que no ven, corazón que no siente.

What the eyes do not see, the heart does not feel.

—*Don Quijote,* Part II, Chapter 67

I live in a time when people love precise terms because such language strokes their terrified minds. The world outside my window is neatly sliced into taxonomic terms. The faces on the streets become job classifications, racial types, legal identification

Why I Wrote This

cards and a growing number of quantifiable disabilities. Physical space is accurately surveyed and demarked by towns, counties, states, and nations. All this is a great comfort in the major work of my particular time on earth: denial.

The very word *Chihuahua* reassures us with its implications of order and exact boundaries and its promise of a distinct content. When I was a schoolboy, my teachers told me that precise terms were necessary for an informed discussion. I believed them then and I do not believe them now. Today, I think the terms, the maps, the charts and the tidy columns of numbers are a drug that lulls us so we do not notice a disintegrating world. Chihuahua, one particular entity, is part of that disintegrating world. We will look at it and thereby obliterate the term itself and for a brief, mescaline-feeling moment, glimpse what it and other tidy boundaries are hiding from our eyes. That is the work at hand and the work will proceed with words and pictures.

This is the story of a place that is not on the maps but is under our feet. This ground is not an imaginary place, nothing has been made up. In a better world, it would be a crime not to record this place on the official maps, but in the world we now live in,

What I Wrote About

such is the case. We have placed urgent calls to the proper authorities pointing out this cartographical felony but so far there has been no response to our objections and no correction of this flagrant error. Under the present circumstances, as you can well imagine, the boundaries of this place are a little hard to pin down. But so are the boundaries of love and no one really doubts the existence of love.

I will tell you what I have had to face, the thing I always knew would come. There will come a spring when the ground smells emerge from the earth, when all around you the sap rises, and when you look up you see the birds pairing and courting. You will know at that moment, life goes on, continues, and does its damnedest to fashion new forms and face new horizons. And yet you will feel a deep fatigue and you will feel you have lost your sense of direction. That moment will be very hard, but you must soldier on because if you will, if you can, then you will taste the thing being born, the very thing that sucks the energy from you and leaves you with a deep sense of fatigue, the very thing that for the moment bobbles that moral compass deep in your gut by whose direction you have always steered your soul. That spring has finally come, and now we must face it and brave it. That is the fact of life in this place. Repeat this word: *Edge*. The sound is a blade that cuts. We must be creatures of faith. What we fear is already upon us, a force launched by birth rates, interest rates, and five hundred years of misdirection, pillage, and neglect. Now we live with it.

Believe that summer follows the spring, then comes the fall and finally winter and it rolls around again, beginning again—but never beginning in exactly the same place. Okay, now we can continue.

The literature on this place is a bit thin—though the evidence of its existence daily grows more overwhelming. The images and words that follow give glimpses of the place the maps fail to acknowledge. Perhaps it is like a favorite tale used to explain chaos theory, the story of the butterfly's wing in Beijing eventually causing a thunderstorm in New York City. Here is the fluttering of a *mariposa*. The storm will arrive in due time.

But then in this hot, dry ground, we always pray for rain.

Shape changer, skinwalker, bruja, *poltergeist,* fantasma, *a shadow on the wall, the feeling of eyes peering through the 2 a.m. window. Something is out there that does not fit the conventional explanations and the officials feel it in their bones, but refuse to say it with their mouths. Undocumented worker? Illegal alien? Wetback? Dryback? Yanqui imperialist? Pinche gringo? Narcotraficante? Refugee? Green card? Free trader? There is constant debate over terms, over what to call this thing moving at the edge of vision, this shape changer. We all feel so much more comfortable with proper terms and better yet, numbers. Technocrats are desperate for both because without proper names and numbers, how can technocrats manage and without managing why in God's name do they even exist? I manage; therefore I am. This fantasy line called the border has a constant thumping of rubbers stamps, and a constant clicking of fingers hitting keys on the computers that will save us all by managing us all. Now and then the secretariat gets a chilling glimpse: a reading off an infra-red screen, aliens moving freely in the cargo bay of a truck and falling on new soil, a statistic in a column of numbers, hummingbirds migrating without papers, a machine pistol chattering in the night, cholera, typhus, all manner of small life forms flowing and drifting without a thought to the regulations, the silent movement of an ice pick. Turn again and it is a* corrido *celebrating a statutory crime, perhaps a whale bobbing dead on the waters, footprints in the wash crossing a line. Then again, it has the look of a flower, a lush beautiful thing blooming color, hypnotizing the eye, flaunting style, oozing sex, and beckoning with lust and love. Yes, a flower, that gaudy sexual thing we use for our weddings and use for our dead and use for our dreams. A rose?*

Imagine the flower, inhale the scent, fear the roots, watch the frightening green leaves rise above us. It begins like the corona of roses framing Our Lady of Guadalupe each December 12, the paper flowers that are the miracle of creation in those last weeks as the sun dies, and then, at solstice chooses to come back again and save our world from darkness. Yes, it begins very simply and safely and within the boundaries of our faith—the roses of Our Lady in December. But something has gone awry, everyone notices this fact. The flowers have become somehow monstrous. They have become blooms beyond our taxonomy. They spread at will, crossing borders, boundaries, all known proprieties. They flourish under bridges, where the barely cool bodies are found in the sands, they burst suddenly into view on city streets, they leave imprints on the desert floor. Their pollen floats over the highest mountains and out over the blue waters. The stems host thorns, but that is not what alarms the authorities. The scent is powerful, almost rank, but also is something the governments can live with, at least they say so.

No it is something else that is frightening them. The novelty of the plant, the fact that it escapes simple taxonomic identification, that reality that no one yet can easily identify and put a name on. This inability to paste a simple label on the thing is driving the officials almost mad. The vigor of the growth also disturbs them—the way this living thing takes on air and water and light, the way it can devour trash and garbage and yet continue to flourish and breed and spread. The very health of the thing is an affront. Worse than the kudzu vine.

Worse than the killer bee. Worse than the screw worm. Worse even than the dreaded narcotics. An alien form without a name, breeding, blooming, spreading. The scent seductive, thorns sharp, roots out of sight but running deeply and sinking into the earth and refusing to let go. No matter what.

Really, there are just two choices left. One is to continue this charade put forth by nations, this act that insists upon the reality of public order, public boundaries, and police. The other is to realize the charade is over. In the short run it is easier to go along with the current unreality. In the long run, it is impossible. So in the end the only real decision is when do we admit to what we see around us. As Joe Louis once noted, you can run but you can't hide.

Not here, not for long.

Tracks, everywhere tracks, marks racing up the arm, footprints pasted against the desert soil, tongues of air moving overhead rich with pollutants, trickles of water coursing down the arroyos or seeping slowly under the earth with their cargos of chemicals and pathogens, spore floating, seeds moving at will in the bellies of birds, everywhere tracks making their imprint and being ignored. That is the fact of this place, the tracks left by constant stampedes, the denial of the tracks by so many observors. Officially, there are many efforts to form links, alliances, relationships across a thing called the border. Governors flit back and forth on their jets to meetings, politicians chow down at various banquets, bureaucrats fax themselves to death in a frenzy of networking. I've done this duty myself, sat there drinking and eating with officials and power brokers hour after hour and bottle after bottle while the bill for lunch rolled upward into the hundreds and hundreds of dollars as we merrily agreed on new relationships between these phantoms, indeed between these two ghost ships, and amused ourselves by calling ourselves nations. This is all the great irrelevancy. The real flow of material and relationships goes on below these official moments.

It is a class thing. The rich and powerful pretend to be in control and pretend to control the flow of things. The poor actually do it. The drugs move, the birds move, the chemicals move, the people move and no one can keep track of these numbers, no one can create an accurate table of these movements, and no one can actually control them. Several days ago at a border checkpoint, an official flagged down a car. The driver of the car accelerated and tried to run down the official. The man in uniform fired on the machine. And here is what happened: the car kept going, raced right through this fantasy they call the border and went on about its errands. No one was arrested. That is what the word border means: a breath of air pretending to be an actual thing. It is finished. The tracks tell us that, the ones on the arm, the ones in the air, the ones on the ground, the ones under the ground. We now are in the edge, the place where big forces rub up against each other, the place beyond the police, past the pretenses of nations. The place where the future has already arrived. There will be no more hit songs about walking the line. Just look at the tracks. Soon a hummingbird will be in my yard from its winter ground in southern Mexico. It will feed and rest and then push on to southern Alaska. We should pay more attention to the birds, *amigos*.

The treaties, the new lease agreements in our global village, are based on the idea that goods can move and capital can move and people stay put. Sixty miles south of my yard they're welding bars against the mouths of the culverts that lance through their magic border. The authorities are apparently creatures of deep faith in their own powers. They are finished I tell you, dinosaurs about to go to their fossil future. Just look at the tracks. They're everywhere, the new bars and all that welding work. Well, let the dreamers dream on a little while longer.

We'll go into the edge. We visit the places of imaginary lines, things with names like say *Chihuahua*. Sometimes they're called Arizona or Sonora or New Mexico or Texas. They look very neat and official. As I said, I have been to meetings, lunches, drunken suppers where these terms and these boundaries were tossed about as absolutes. But out on the ground things are moving, always moving, scuttling along in the night and in the day. And they defy these notions. Tracks, everywhere tracks. And brilliant colors. The thing itself is too new for our minds to wrap it up in a tidy package. But its presence can be detected—the tracks, the colors.

Let's go.

Colors stream into the mind from the Mexican walls. Burnt orange, blood red, dark green, rich blues, deep purple, turquoise, yellow, pink, and black. Big solid swatches of color that dress a business, a house, a shack. The road from Ojinaga on the river to

What I Wrote

Ciudad Chihuahua is stone, dust, dun colored hills but the marks of people protest this drabness and scream out colors. The colors are innocent, naive, and arrogant. They refuse to apologize and are never shy. Beneath the high desert mask of Chihuahua beats a gaudy heart and from this throbbing organ flows the colors of passions and blurted thoughts. It is the easiest thing to notice and the first thing noticed and the thing always remembered. For a North American it is almost like discovering the spoken word or music, an explosive shout that in the nation to the north is either forbidden or feared or forgotten.

We have invented a jagged line that crosses deserts and mountains and valleys and rivers. This line is the first expression of the edge visible to the eye. We stare into the face of pain. We look into a mouth of broken teeth, these stubs called things like Baja, Sonora, Chihuahua. Once the north of the Spanish Empire reached above San Francisco Bay, into Arizona and New Mexico, across the span of Texas and beyond. This grandeur was in part an illusion—a terrain largely empty, often out of royal control and here and there studded with presidios, fortress like ranch headquarters, embattled mining districts. Over the course of three centuries, Spain established a presence in this north, not a control. Strange names floated back to the capital, *Apache, Comanche, Tarahumara, Yaqui,* and the ever useful term for barbarians— *Chichimec.* There were sixteenth-century forays like Coronado's trek toward seven fabled cities of gold, various voyages, slave raids, and now and then huge leaps into nowhere to found colonies and military outposts. None of these efforts were cost effective and they tended to leave better histories than communities. On the ground the northern advance stalled in the sixteenth century and then in the seventeenth and eighteenth centuries made kangaroo leaps based on the discovery of mineral pockets. By the time of the Mexican-American War ignorance of the area was still great enough that the imperial schemes of the North Americans forced them to come back for a second bite (the Gadsden Purchase) when the first conquest failed to include a decent railroad route through the desert ground. This place, the edge, remains the great known unknown, something impaled on maps like a butterfly but wild and free on the ground. It's the home place for all those rejected by the decent homes, the refugee center for Mexicans and North Americans. None of this is admitted by the authorities but increasingly no one wishes to talk to them anyway. In the beginning, the color was blue in the sky, brown in the dirt, red in the violence, and gold in the dreams. But colors always, colors.

Cross an imaginary line drawn in the dirt and backed by heat sensors, wire, guns, and law and suddenly pass from a world numbed by beige, teal, pastels, and other mild hues to one primal, primary, and violent in tone. A mere detail, many would agree compared to the serious consequences of the historical record, the implications of free trade, the obligations and curses of the First World facing the Third World. Maybe so.

But open your eyes and tell me that.

That is how it begins, with colors dripping off walls and rolling down the streets, pouring into the arroyos, surging against the banks of rivers. Colors shouting so loudly that at first you cannot hear the distant thunder of the revolutions, the bells of the colonial past, the drums of the tribes, the bleating of academics scouting post-modernism or post-colonialism. Just the brush full of colors lapping against your face. And after a while the colors cease to be an assault and become something you feel is normal like love or song or good food or a caress.

I am walking down the street toward the start of Saturday evening in Ciudad Chihuahua. Couples are clambering off the cheap buses, the ones with dirty windows or broken windows. The men are in clean jeans, boots, and elaborately stitched shirts that enjoy every color except white. They all but become invisible next to their women in sheer materials, daring necklines, brilliant hues of blue, green, red, purple, high heels with acrylic surfaces, and faces defined by dark coronas around the eyes, long lashes, flashing finger nails, blazing lips. They promenade under the stunted trees by the sleeping market, a band plays, and yet hardly anyone speaks. They simply are . . . moving columns of color.

A taco stand hosts three tall stools before its little counter, and alone on the center stool with her back to me, a woman in a red dress with long black hair leans forward toward her plate, her one leg akimbo to reach a bar on which to rest her high heel, and I stop and look at the color, the curves, the ease of her body language as the light dies and night comes on and still the colors refuse to leave.

> *He is born in the Sierra Madre of Chihuahua, where trees and grass grow and the winters can bring a killing cold. His father has a little rancho. They run some stock, raise some corn, get by somehow. When the marijuana and narcotraficantes invade the sierra, Ernesto's father is not interested. So at a fiesta, they kill his father. And Ernesto in turn kills a man for this murder. He flees deeper into the sierra. He is thirteen.*

We live in a world that does not know its own name. The form of some word rolls around in our mouths, a jagged piece of lava we wish to smooth, but we cannot make sounds come. A taste bites into our tongues, a frightening flavor seeping off that jagged rock, but still the sounds do not come and all we have is that taste and that taste is failure.

A dead whale bobs on the waters of the desert sea, hundreds of dolphins rot on the beaches as the experts scamper to decide what caused this dying, and the nations slowly pivot their attention from the concerns of distant capitals and for a few seconds consider who is to blame and is the cause natural or unnatural and is the cause Mexican or American and is . . . and then they forget about it, as they always do because it all happens on ground that burns and heaves beyond the limits of their attention. A place on a map but surely not within the throb of their national lives. Gulls scream overhead, faxes purr out of machines, the vast bureaucracies of order lumber on, and still the whales bob in the sea, an enormous mass of dead flesh too small to sustain the attention of the creatures sitting at desks and staring into the dead eyes of computers. I have lived like the whale, in a world beneath notice.

We are barbarians, creatures who live beyond the civilized, the Germans skulking in the forest across the Rhine of the Caesars, the Mongols on their runty horses barred by the Great Wall, savage Scots stopped by Hadrian's barrier. A world of checkpoints, fences, heat sensors, agents, spies, forms. Those without manners, the Chichimec, the outlaws, the psychopaths hitchhiking and leaving death and anonymous ruin in our wake. Barbarians in a world still being born, jagged lava in mouths, creatures held in contempt, orphans of a hot ground. We are said to be regulated: by fences, guns, laws, satellites high in the sky that look over our shoulders constantly. But we refuse to know this fact. The flesh moves at will, people walking through wires and walls as if these barriers did not exist. Marijuana, heroin, and cocaine are delivered more promptly than truckloads of tomatoes. And in the air, invisible to the eye, money moves, torrents of money, rivers of money, oceans of money. The green sea flows this way and that way and no one commands or controls it. The governments, they pretend to be the masters of this flow but they are not. A verdin flits from bloom to bloom on the chuperosa out my window and the money crackles through the air, billions and billions of dollars and pesos, crackling and shrieking, and no one can control it. We are to be regulated, it is said in all the newspapers and on the dusty screens of our televisions. The marijuana is good this year, the money roars past, the people move at will. We are barbarians and now beyond control.

We used to know our place. I remember as a boy the absolute reality of maps. I could jab my finger at a spot, some crossroads or hamlet, and know at that very instant people were drinking coffee, gathering gossip, driving fence posts, or making machines. I could look at a dot and imagine a type of house, a favorite brand of tea on a shelf in the kitchen, a local team followed by all during the sweet months of summer. I was struck as a boy how simple things like the heft of coffee mugs in a

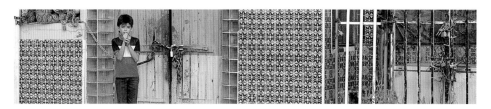

country cafe or the cut of side meat at breakfast would differ according to an exact place. The way women painted their faces varied also. Now at times, I think only the dogs know their place. When I was a boy we took a country kid along to our apartment in a big city and I remember him craning his neck out the rear window of the car to take in his first skyscraper—a building six stories tall. Just as I remember at age seven or eight being in Mexico and my astonishment at restaurants that did not serve real food and markets that had merchants sprawled out on the pavement. Such a pull of a locale is notoriously waning under the beam of satellite television and under the wanderings induced by growing unemployment. In a world of sojourners, everyone gets to visit about the world but no one ever really sinks roots into this bigger world. In a way, résumés have replaced genealogies; football jerseys and t-shirts from rock concerts have supplanted local efforts at costume. But all this mass marketing of goods and human beings has disguised what I feel under the surface and taste in my mouth and what dances across my eyes. The emergence of a place beneath the maps of nations and beneath the consciousness of rulers. A place still beneath the language of the very people who live in it. But this place I speak of is actual. It has a form and ethos and, when the light is right and the eye is cocked, a definition that is growing sharper and sharper as it looms out of the dust storms that rake my world.

We, not an imperial *we* but a compassionate and inclusive *we,* live in this new thing we have so much trouble saying. They try to confuse us with floods of goo and noise flowing down various information highways, but this distraction cannot in the long run deny us our new birth right. We will say the word and then it will be actual. The room will change with our sounds just as an insult converts a Saturday afternoon cantina into a new and ferocious beast. To be more exact now would not be wise. The storm still rages, the rivers still rise, and the exact geography will come with the dawn when we can in clear light see the new channels gouged, the soils deposited, the islands standing on the brows of volcanoes in the sea, the mountains squeezed up from the worlds buried beneath us. Then we can take our measure. No one in power will help us. The very thing happening is what is being denied by the rhetoric of the nations. They are like the aged when they feel death's hand on their shoulders—at some level aware of this coldness but determined to deny this thing, this inevitable thing. We will know our place.

We are said to be a border but a border requires a real solid object, say a nation —we cannot be the border of phantoms. But our Ultimo Thule is collapsing, a morning fog now being burned off before our eyes. We constitute the border of a dying order. We have become something else, something new because we are not dying, we are being born.

The wind rises and is dry, the sun hunts with a white light, our lips crack, dust settles on the surface of our catatonic eyes. We move through the shadows—we are the refugees, illegals, bastards. All of us have come as far from something as we can possibly go and still we wish to press on. Someday we will focus our eyes, the jagged rock in our mouth will be smoothed, and then this ground will shake and a hawk will wheel in the sky and scream.

We live on the edge. Yes, that is it, the edge. The place where we live. Day by day, the jagged rock cuts, our tongues bleed, yet the stone grows slowly smoother. The taste, that taste so powerful that nothing can rinse it from our mouths—not coffee or tequila, not tea, not whiskey—the taste of failure sours with our fears, bitters with our disappointments. So for the moment, the edge it is. We are jittery, unsure, angry, and alert. We place bars on our windows, guns in our hands, chemicals in our bodies, and refuse to read all the new laws that spread like slime mold on the statute books. We sense a new language growing in our minds, a weedy expanse of sounds and words. The vowels will be full, the cadence stately, and everything in this language will ride securely on a solid bass line, a sinuous guitar, and a coke-driven snare drum. Everyday as we go about our tasks we can feel this edge before our face, a jagged lip gaping just where we are about to step, and vertigo is our sense of balance.

But soon, soon, the center. When the words finally come, when the lava grows a bit smoother, then the sounds will surge forth from our now strangled throats. Not the Northwest of Mexico, the Southwest of the United States. Not states with useless

They bag 900 on a Tuesday and brag of a new record.

*They pounce on a thousand two days later and boast that this
proves their system is working.*

*A horse train with 2400 pounds is detected, the arrest
a mere blip on the big blank screen of the authorities.*

*I am reading to five-year-olds in a kindergarten class and
I pause and ask, "How many of you have been on a farm?"
The eager brown faces shout back, "Un rancho, si!"*

names, the Arizona, the Sonora, the New Mexico, the Chihuahua, the unloved west fragment of Texas. Not nations. They use us but are useless to us. We are leaving the nations and they know it. Their police are everywhere but this show of force is to no avail. They are building metal walls and we laugh at these efforts as we stare out the windows through our useless iron bars. We will cease to live in relation to distant capitals. We will realize we are defending the wrong border. For now, the edge is a jittery place full of heat, color, gore, change, collision, and lust. A cauldron from which the center will come forth. Our tongues lick, the lava cuts. They are hiring more and more police but they will fail also. Checkpoints keep increasing. El Paso, Albuquerque, Phoenix, Tucson, Ciudad Juarez, Hermosillo, Ciudad Chihuahua and all the *Desemboques*. Not a nation, not a politics, not even a word yet. We press on, being born, bleeding, listening to all the jukeboxes as the choppers whomp over our heads and flash the spotlights in the night.

So many years of meetings where someone will say the boundary is drawn by the use of adobe as a building material, or the boundary is drawn by the extent of a Spanish Empire or of an American Empire. Sometimes plants are recruited to stand sentinel on vaunted borders. Others demand rivers toiling all along the watch towers. There are commissions, hands across borders, twin factory plans, strange agreements that make trade free and the edge a free fire zone. My head has ached for years with these meetings about defining a region, these books about the essence and strict limits of the world I live in and refuse to leave. One day I gave up on such discussions. I felt the jagged rock in my mouth, faced up to the blood on my tongue, sensed the sounds struggling up from my throat. I took a large map off the wall, struck a match and watched flames first lick its edges and then race across the babble of its mountains and rivers and valleys and place names. When it cooled, I swept up the ashes and threw them in the trash can.

Edge. The place we live. The place I live. The places the future lives as the lava slowly smoothes. No one notices us at the moment and this is good. The authorities are all so busy with their treaties and commissions and metal walls and heat sensors and paramilitary units. Communiqués flit through a cyberspace where the doddering nations delicately delineate their virtual reality. We are beneath comment. We move on hard ground under a savage sun and we grow and grow within the metes and bounds of their fantastic schemes. The nations have policies, we have hungers. And our hungers will take us to the future and leave them in the past. We are barbarians and this will protect us from them until it is too late to stop us. That is when the center will come into being, when the words will pour forth from us. But for now, our tongues keep licking and licking that jagged lava. For now, a secret universe is so alive the maps deny it exists.

> *He tumbles down the barrancas that rake into the western side of Chihuahua. He is often hungry and confused. The ground is huge canyons, rivers that roar through gorges. Strange birds. Terrible climbs. His feet are sore and he meets Indians. He keeps dropping down until he is on the hot coastal plain. If he turns back, he will be killed and he knows this fact. But to go forward is to venture into a world he does not know. When he finally reaches a port on the Pacific, he is no longer a boy.*

The Old World first comes to the page in Chaucer and then trills through the centuries as the edge of something—a town, a cemetery, a flowerbed. That is the track of the word *border* in our language. The New World gives the word a new edge, a sharpness and danger that drips blood like a Bowie knife. James Fenimore Copper in his 1827 novel, *Prairie,* notes, "The indirect manner so much in use by the border inhabitants." And then the danger of the word accelerates in the United States and by 1863 abolitionist Wendell Phillips is booming from the public platform, "He put a guard at every Border-ruffian's door." The sound covers the space past civilization, that jittery ground beyond the frontier. By 1870, American mining engineer Raphael Pumpelly simply jots down, "a border bully, armed with revolver, knife and rifle." Later on, when in a lucky moment, he stops a thug from murdering him, his would-be assailant eyes him coldly and announces, "You'll do for the border."

The weaponry has remained fairly constant—the bolt action rifle replaced by the machine pistol, the knives at times giving way to the ice pick—but the potency of the word has grown darker and darker as the physical border has become frailer and frailer. The authorities talk of guarding the border but no one in my world lives on the border. Now we live within it, the fumes rising from the molten lava, the earth shaking, the signs and wires and flags snapping off the posts, comic touches to our days and nights. Mexico now has more mouths than the ground there can feed. The United States will have 560 million people in sixty years and they will limp

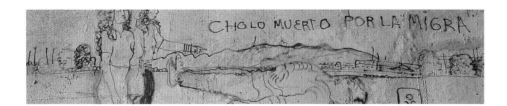

across a landscape of burned-out soil, exhausted oil fields, dead or deadly rivers, and vanished aquifers. Still the governments talk of the border as if it were real or for that matter, as if they were real. But we know they increasingly are not. They are ghosts, shadowy things haunting someplace faraway. We refuse to look at them. When we are in the Mexican North, we look north. When we are in what the government calls the American Southwest, we look south. We are beginning to mumble to each other. We are beginning to realize we are trapped on a dry and burning pan of dirt and it is not the border but our future world.

I am sitting in a cafe twenty feet from the fence. A small glass of tequila, a gratuity of this establishment, rests on the table before me and I look north from a place called Mexico into a place called the United States. For much of my life I seriously believed the border existed and I believed it was exactly as wide as the wire I now look at. I even believed in the border when I wandered on foot in places where the fence did not exist and my only clue to this passage between nations would be pock marks on the ground marking the sensors of the authorities. For years there has been a different theory, one that a third nation, a very skinny nation, was emerging on the border, a country ten, twenty, thirty, forty miles wide and longer than any snake ever found in the natural world. I have never believed this theory because I have always been struck by the absoluteness of the fence, by the total difference in language and custom that simply stepping across the wire brought instantly to my attention. Now I have, well, mellowed. I do not believe in the border, nor in this would-be skinny nation. I now live on a large island, one the maps disguise as Sonora, Chihuahua, a chunk of Texas, and most of Arizona and New Mexico. This is the place of the edge, the ground where the power of the nations recedes and the drive of the human beings accelerates. It is largely a hot and dry place, brown is the basic color, and here and there big mountains rise up and wave green knobs at the sky. When I go from Phoenix to say Salt Lake City, I leave the edge. When I wander north from Albuquerque to Denver, I am no longer in it either. But if I bumble down to Hermosillo or Ciudad Chihuahua I am still on my home ground.

The cafe where I sit with my tequila is part of a bungled effort to insist on order and fine edges in this place where I live. I have just ridden a bicycle on a tour called from border to border, by which the planners meant from one side of a state to the other side where this place called Mexico officially is said to begin. Now the trip is over, and I sit and have a drink. Every minute as I sit there, people go through a big hole in the fence just twenty feet away and then they walk north into the fabled United States. Two blocks away is the official customs house and a man I've known for years sits there on a high stool and officially decides who in the endless line officially crossing the official border can officially proceed. I am watching more business at this one hole, than this man on the high stool ever handles. The authorities have posted a video camera high on a pole and it patiently sweeps to and fro along the fence. The people climbing through the hole and heading north carefully time their moves off the sweep of this camera. A block away is a house where drugs are stored. I once met a fellow who moved a huge load of drugs through this hole, a few kilos at a time, simply by timing the scurrying of his employees off the endless rounds of this high-tech guard dog. Of course, when from time to time I talk to the authorities and mention these matters, they nod and tell me this is simply a minor flaw in their grand concept of the border, a tiny tear in the fabric and they will soon get around to mending this hole. And of course, they do, and then five or ten or a hundred more holes pop up. This never seems to faze them or rock their religious faith in the border. They will have none of my notion of the edge.

But I live in some kind of dream world, I suspect, where forces operate that the authorities do not believe even exist. For example, on this recently completed bike safari, one rider braked by a dead raven on the road, plucked a black feather and rode on. He had five flat tires that day. I knew he would. I never mess with ravens, although I can't claim that they are that nice to me. I've had them bop me on my skull, loot my camps, and hover just overhead screaming obscenities at me. They are territorial, they mate for life. They've made it perfectly obvious they consider me a fool and they mock the very idea of a border. They are truly creatures of the edge.

The power of the dry land is also an element of the edge. Sometimes I read books about the flora and fauna where this power is chipped away at and enslaved in fine taxonomic manacles. But this tactic only works temporarily, just as all these illegal drugs only work for a short while. The key facts about my ground are that it is so immense it swallows you up no matter how big you think you are, and that it is insidious, so insidious that after you have been here a while you are never able to leave despite the miserable wages, the bad governments, the endless police hassles, the limited water, and the summers that hunt you each day like a contract killer.

So that is it: tequila, holes in the fence, demonic ravens, ground as addictive as cocaine, and the edge.

> *Somehow he works his way up to Los Angeles. The story is vague here, but somehow he does this. He learns a trade, let's say upholstery and laying carpet. He buys false papers which is not hard for him to do. He works, saves, is, according to the documents in his pocket, an American. Once he goes to his job and sees immigration raiding the place. He turns around and never goes back. There are plenty of jobs for someone such as he.*

They loom ahead on the flat hot pan of earth, rise up like huge monoliths. Almost always they are in ruins, beached creatures from a time when a different sea ran here. They are the haciendas of Chihuahua, grotesque buildings where once fabled grandees held their sway over herds of peasants. Usually, a village squats by them, a collective hamlet called an *ejido*, one of the social experiments created by the Mexican Revolution that opened the twentieth century with a fine fury. Sometimes chickens peck on the floors of the empty rooms. Always the windows stare out blindly and without glass. It interests me that in a nation without housing or money, no one ever seems to live in these big old houses. And no one among the modern rich ever seems to reclaim one, gussy it up, and move back in. The structures seem to have a curse on them and so I always find them in ruins with the huts of the poor huddled around them, carrion birds feeding on the blubber of these beached whales.

They are a product of the great cattle empires that Spain created as a way of probing north into the other darkness called Chichimeca, the land of the barbarians.

These almost medieval estates were to create order from the chaos of a frontier. Instead they seem to have bred yet more barbarians. W. B. Yeats warned us about this mansion thing:

> The intellect of man is forced to choose
> Perfection of the life, or of the work.
> And if it takes the second must raise
> A heavenly mansion, raging in the dark.

A priest named Arregui peered north into this ground, this place of the edge, in the seventeenth century and noted, "There is so much uninhabited space in these realms that I doubt whether Europe's entire population could fill them; not only do they have no known boundaries, but all or nearly all is empty." In those days, it took three, maybe four months in the dry season to travel from Mexico City to the southern edge of Chihuahua. Now, of course, the trip takes much less time but the distance between the capital and this ground seems to be increasing. Into this empty ground, Spain put cattle and men to own the cattle and other men to work the cattle. A peculiar culture emerged: horsemen galloping about with *desjarretaderas,* crescent shaped blades mounted on long poles. With these weapons, the men would deftly hamstring a bull. They also used these tools against other men. Soon these horsemen were busy rustling the cattle. As early as 1574, the desjarretardera was outlawed. Nobody paid any attention to this regulation, the sixteenth century equivalent of modern gun control. By 1607, a royal inspector complained of this new element, "especially the mestizos, mulattos, and free Negroes: they are called saddletree lads because their sole possessions are a wretched old saddle, a lightly stepping mare (stolen), and their harqebus or short lance." When the North Americans blundered into the region much later, they would confront a similar experience: men gone free and wild once they reached the edge. Back in the sixteenth century, another Spanish inspector observed that "they strike terror in the heart of the population, calling themselves vaqueros, they ride about armed with desjarretadera, or scythes; they collect in bands and no one dares withstand them."

For centuries these men would be the fodder in various revolts and bouts of outlawry. They would come to be the self-image of the ground, the wildness of a Chihuahua where, a former governor noted in the 1920s, the principal problem of the place was that there were too many men who could accurately fire a rifle at one hundred yards. Wherever I wander in the edge, I still stumble into these men in bars and restaurants and cantinas and deserts and sierras. They casually clutch their machine pistols or carelessly stuff a .9 mm in their back pants pocket and continue to go about their business blissfully unimpressed by all notions of borders. Living in the emptiness has filled many human souls. For centuries, the authorities in both nations have viewed this culture of vaqueros or outlaws or rebels as a temporary annoyance to be resolved by a new policy or program or firing squad. To date, they have not made a dent. Order seems to remain a prisoner of the maps and barely visible on the ground itself.

The dead whales of Chihuahua are monuments to this quest for order. These rotting hulks stare out as huge scars marking the fury of the wild men with their long scythes. General Francisco Villa himself finally retired from all his killing to just such a mansion in Canutillo, a hop-skip-and-a-jump over the line in the state of Durango. He turned the place into a communal village and settled in with his soldiers. I've visited there: the big house is in part a museum to the general and the bloody revolution. But much of it, including Villa's own quarters are in ruins with rats and birds defecating in the various chambers. As I said, there is a curse on these establishments. For a small fee an old man will unlock the two maintained rooms in the old hacienda where bric-a-brac and photographs from the days of the revolution are displayed much as the bones of saints are kept in a room in a church. I stare into a huge blowup of Villa's army swirling through a cloud of dust in battle while a *campesino* on a tired horse clomps past just outside the museum as he goes to work his field. It is all very offhanded, this museum, in part I suspect because what it is supposed to contain still roams freely outside its cloistered walls.

Woodrow Wilson casually told a French military attaché in December 1914, "Villa today represents the only instrument of civilization in Mexico. His firm authority allows him to create order, and to educate the turbulent mass of peons so prone to pillage." You see it never seems to stop, this sense of dread about the people of the edge and this pious dream that somehow we can be gelded, trained to the saddle and ridden. For the rulers of both nations, we are the dark dream that awakens them in the night to find their sheets soaked with sweat and provokes them to fantasies of control. For centuries, they have dreaded our scythes and fancied schemes in which we will beat these blades into some sort of plowshares. This is the fatal addiction of power, the true cocaine of our world in which the rulers snort the white powder in their distant citadels and roar that they will not let us exercise our will but will impose their ways on our ways.

John Lind, a drunken special representative of President Wilson's to Villa's ragtag Army of the North, filed this message to his president during the revolution: "We must be a pillar of cloud by day and the pillar of fire by night and compel decent administration. From this necessity there is no escape, unless revolution and anarchy are to continue to be the order of the day in Mexico. Let this housecleaning be done by home talent. It will be a little rough, and we must see to it that the walls are left intact, but I should not worry if some of the verandahs and French windows were demolished. General Villa, for instance, would do the job satisfactorily."

I walk into General Villa's room at his hacienda and truly the windows are demolished. The roof too has collapsed and out the door local villagers sit in the shade and lean against the crumbling walls and talk with drunken merriment. I know at this very moment in distant capitals new presidents think they control these men and that they can direct them and that maybe a few French windows will get smashed but in the end, order and civilization will prevail. You see, the border will be shored up—a wall here, a few thousand troops there, heat sensors underfoot, spy satellites overhead, special dogs with exquisitely tuned snouts everywhere—economies will be grown like cannabis in a greenhouse, trade will boom, the environment will be cleansed thanks to new riches, populations will learn various computer languages, loins will go cold with family planning lectures, and all will be well . . . once the minor adjustments of the current unpleasantness are behind us. A bird lands over my head on a rotting beam and I stare up through the collapsed room at the burning blue sky in the ruins of General Villa's chamber. He once told a woman, "For me the war began when I was born." Now he is dead and gone, his grave looted, his head stolen. He is a memory, like the haciendas themselves, a phantom to be no doubt easily erased from consciousness by the might of the new order of free trade and factories and special passports and high technology and currency reforms and all the rest of the cybernetic package.

But still the whales have a haunting quality, dead desert whales that once were so mighty and now serve as chicken coops and pigeon roosts and pigsties and junk-yards. The car stops in a dirt lane before a small house. The caretaker comes out, smiles, and says sure. I get out and walk toward the parapets of another Chihuahuan hacienda. The walls are red from the clay of the local ground and the ruin floats on a sea of brown grass and mesquite trees. To the east, the grasslands fall away as the desert bites in hard and dry and when I turn that direction I stare into the distant maw of the Bolson de Mapima, a forbidding country where rebels and vaqueros have always felt safe from authorities. Villa and his soldiers would cross the Bolson like Bedouins navigating a kind of Mexican Sahara. The ruined hacienda is huge with a rounded and melting tower of mud on one corner. I climb through a hole in the old wall, enter the courtyard. A small chapel nails down one corner, the family quarters take the L of another. Like all the other whales, the old building exudes a stench of defeat. I clamber up an old stairway and stand on the roof and confront the melting walls of what once must have constituted the village of the grandees and campesinos. I do not try to imagine what it was like when it was alive. I lack the stomach for such a fantasy of power and greed and cruelty. There is a persistent vice in my hot dry ground of imagining fabled times when big houses hosted noble men and women who ruled as a fine aristocracy over a dumb but congenial local population. Many feed off these visions. I prefer to think of the curved blades on long poles, of wild boys riding stolen mares into the dust.

Down in the hacienda's courtyard a stele rises up. It is almost a thumb in my eye but I am drawn to it. Carved in it is the name of someone who was born around 1900 but died around 1920. No doubt the respectable son of a respectable house mowed down by the savagery of all the Villas who stalked this land. The slab says the young man died in defense of order. The top has been busted off the monument and lies nearby in the weeds. Jimson weed grows in the roofless rooms now.

All I can hear is the wind blowing. This place is dead. But the idea keeps coming back. It seems inevitable. Surely, order can be established here. Neat lines on a map, police with shined shoes, civil laws. It has all been simply a failure to communicate. The jimson weed seems to be flourishing and soon no doubt it will bloom with a ghastly white flower beckoning the moon and all its psychoactive juices will surge through its tissues. A mere cup of tea made from the plant can render a man insensible and push his notions of order into total insanity. The plants are flourishing all around the stele. The haciendas, the old whales are rotting away. The jimson weed, the sacred datura, is casting down seed.

It's all right here if you want it, all the messages and warnings and joyous shouts, here in the dusty abandoned dead courtyard, here, right here on the edge.

It is not clear where the drugs come in but it is clear why they come in: money. By his late teens or early twenties, he is selling drugs and going back and forth to Mexico. He meets people like Raphael Caro Quintero, and he becomes a trusted member of the business. He wears a holy medallion, attends parties, moves loads, sometimes kills people. And he does not get caught. He is very alert, very smart. He starts a small business on the North American side and earns money from helping out in a big business on the Mexican side. He lives in a fine house in the States and is serious about getting ahead.

They come through the gaps in the mountains, course down the dry valleys, follow the dirt tracks to my door. Costas, rufous, annas, broad-bills, black-chinned—big clouds of hummingbirds. Mallards, red heads, buffleheads, blue-winged teals, American wigeons, endless Vs of ducks. Orioles, tanagers, long strands of colorful songbirds. The killers are always hot on their trails—red-tail hawks, golden eagles, peregrine falcons, kestrels, great horned owls. Coyotes, rattlesnakes, badgers, raccoons. There are fangs waiting everywhere around where I live. I'm only four or five miles from the border and so there are also lots of cops—deputy sheriffs, DEA, Border

Patrol, Army, all tucked away behind bushes and waiting for prey. I see them often in the gray light of morning when I stand on the porch in the freezing air and piss while they lock on me with their powerful optics.

Still, it seems very peaceful and there are a lot of lazy afternoons for aimless talk. When Ted came out, we had all the time in the world. He drove the seven miles of bad dirt road, made it through the two gates and dropped down into my private valley. His Stetson was old and stained and the hat band was lined with rolled joints like a bandoleer. He'd been in the game for a good twenty-five years—he showed me an old photo of a military jet a hundred feet off the deck and roaring just above the top of his teepee. He'd beaten all the raps. That time when they seized his briefcase stuffed with a hundred grand at the airport, why he simply refused to admit it was his and he walked away from the money and the waiting prison cell. Of course, after that he dropped the front he was running, a nursery. He no longer ran loads of bougainvillea to Los Angeles, each shrub surrounded by the world's most expensive soil amendment.

He's a burly guy with a quick and witty tongue and after he lights up another joint, he gets even more talkative. He recently had a load break down right by my front gate on the maimed country road that is crowded with the war wagons of the cops. This did not seem to phase him—he simply called a wrecker and had the truck and its six hundred pound load towed to his house. The choppers that are constantly overhead don't give him much concern either, nor do the hopeless DEA plants that hang out at the small saloon. In fact, where I live there really isn't much of a war on drugs but more of a war game where no one seems to get hurt, except accidentally. I remember when the two DEA guys asked me what I was doing out in that lonely valley and I said, "I watch birds." I think my comment got me on some kind of special list. The place itself is kind of a sore point with them. I'm sure they still remember the time they raided it—had to cut the gate off with a torch—and couldn't find the marijuana field. It was right across the arroyo up in the mesquites and was wonderfully nurtured by a drip irrigation system. About the only sign of that visit are the big numbers they pasted on the gate post. The SWAT team, it seems, had a hell of a time finding the place.

I tell Ted my map idea. We'll create a map showing all of the smuggling routes, and lord, they're old, some going back a century or more with ruts worn deep in the stone from the mule trains. I point out that both sides know the routes, so it's not like we'll be giving away proprietary information when we publish this baby and let the world in on both the game and comic aspects of this non-Olympic sanctioned sport. My only request is that every route make a detour to the DEA headquarters so that a donation can be made to their retirement fund. His eyes light up at the notion and I haul down my 7.5 and 15 minute topographical charts and he begins rattling off the geography of drug smuggling. His finger races over mesas, down hopeless canyons, through grassy saddles, and across dry burning flats. His mind is electric with the delight of defining and publicizing this playground where he makes a living and the authorities crank a couple of hundred million a year through their budgets and everyone, literally everyone, still gets stoned. Of course, like any game, there are rules. The local band he fronts has six members but almost always only plays with five because some one has been benched in a state or federal joint for a spell.

Ted plucks another joint from his hat band and lights up. He's a natural leader kind of guy and I can tell the notion of printing up this special map appeals to his sense of civic duty. We're all North Americans here and public service is an ideal deeply rooted in our hearts. I can hear the ducks quacking down the hill at the pond, see a swarm of hummingbirds at my feeders—they're guzzling a quart a day of sugar water. Hooded orioles and summer tanagers are frolicking in my bird bath. They are all part of a migration that's been going on for millions of years, one fueled by appetites so deep that it is unlikely that any human definition of the border will ever give this vast wave of energy the slightest pause.

While Ted is sketching away his AAA guide I pour myself a glass of wine. I ask him a simple question, "Ted, they've got to know what you are up to, especially after that bad day at the airport with the briefcase. Don't you ever worry about them watching your house?"

He looks up at me with his bright eyes and says, "Ah, shit yes. I see them all the time through the scope on my rifle."

"You're not going to shoot one are you?"

"You think I'm fucking crazy?" he replies as he looks at me with bewilderment. "I shoot one on my own property and they can RICO me, seize all my fucking assets. Hell, I'd never do that. But Christ, I see'm all the time through my scope out there in the bushes. Must be a hell of a cold, hungry way to live, don't you think?"

Domestic corn production in the United States is $11 billion; the soybean production is $14 billion. Domestic marijuana weighs in at about $32 billion, constituting at most one-half of the level of consumption in the United States. And yet the authorities still insist on the idea of a border. And the culture still insists on calling the drug world a marginal creature, a kind of special darkness kept at the edge of town. We all pretty much insist on this fact. It is part of a mental package of straight lines on the map, tidy procedures, strict protocols, visas, checkpoints, and other stigmata of order. The same mouth that can say Chihuahua and see this well-defined entity can also shout the international border and believe what it says. But on the ground, in the places where no one bothers reading maps, things simply flow—drugs, people, birds, whatnot. Always, I watch the birds with their indifference to our notions of boundaries and our obliviousness to the movement of birds. It could be argued that global ecocide has only come to our attention because of the teaching of birds—negative lessons driven home when come spring in a dark year they fail to arrive as scheduled because some other piece of their world has been obliterated by our hungry hands. All these clues are papered over by our increasing insistence on this thing called a border, an insistence voiced in treaties, commissions, military units, studies, and fine, colorful maps. Of course, I am blind to these claims and studies and see at best an edge, a grinding locale of energy and fury that lives by its own rules and busily invents its own future.

Ted and I still haven't finished that map but when we do, I predict, it'll revolutionize the game and get us sanctioned by the college athletic associations, at least the small ones. The authorities keep refining the rules—Blackhawk choppers, ground sensors, night-vision optics, new bladed border roads—but it really doesn't alter the game. We've both got too much invested in the sport to give up on it or have it ruined. Like all living things, our sap rises with the season.

His carpet business in the states does well, he has employees and now a yet finer house looking out over the city lights. Eventually, his luck takes a little tumble and the authorities get their fingers on his throat. He flips, becomes an informant, and sends some of his colleagues to jail. And he keeps doing drug deals all the while. He ignores death threats, moves about publicly. There are irritations. Once I am to meet him at a bar. He does not show up. He was detained by an effort to burn his business to the ground. Still, he professes no fear. And he raises the fees he charges the authorities for information.

He has been watching me ever since I came into the bar. His car is parked outside, I can see it through the huge glass windows. It is a red sports car with a red-leather hood screen. There cannot be many such cars in Parral, an old city with many bridges huddled against the winds in the south of Chihuahua. Villa used to visit this town often. During the revolution, he'd roar in to shake down the rich so he could finance his army. After the revolution, he'd roar in to buy supplies, sleep with women, and tend to his various enterprises. He was murdered here on July 20, 1923. But now Parral is floating like so much of this ground, floating toward a future that seems to be near but cannot be clearly determined. The man who is eyeing me might be part of that future. He finally comes over and talks, stressing how his city has many fine ladies. He is very friendly and would like to help me meet some of these fine ladies. He says he runs a health club. He wears a lot of gold chains and loves to shop in the United States, where everything is fine. Parral, he explains, is pretty boring. I assume he is a drug dealer, but who knows? Perhaps, Parral is a hotbed of fitness freaks.

The hotel I am staying at has two discotheques. One is housed in the main building, a windowless room with booming sound, flashing lights, and well-dressed women who are young and restless. But next door is the larger edifice. It is a castle complete with turrets. I forget the admission charge now, but a bottle of scotch goes for sixty bucks. The rich of Parral flock here to celebrate being rich. In the evening I look out my hotel window and watch them queue up. These discos are the new haciendas, the new fortresses of power. Their walls deny the might of those darker, poorer people, the problem people that order will finally tame or erase.

My new friend has other friends. A group of ranchers who sit and drink for hours and stare out the big windows at Parral. They are the descendants of the fabled grandees who once lived in the big haciendas. They tick off the names of estates and mansions like beads on a rosary. Like so many on this ground, they despise the distant capital and the rulers who live there and think they can rule here. All their attention is directed to a different direction, to the north and the big money that is found *otro lado,* on the other side. They are the sharks of this sea. They are too wise to believe in whales or wish to be a whale. They know everything about moving money and secret accounts and bookkeeping tricks.

I listen to their loud talk and I recall one night in Ciudad Chihuahua when I was walking late at night and passed two Tarahumara women sprawled out in the doorway of a closed store near the cathedral. One woman looked up at me briefly and then demanded, "Hey, give me money."

You can get lost in this talk of money and economies and policies and poverty. The thing to remember, I decide, is that the discos look like castles. The thing to remember when you live in the edge is that the search for order is a permanent condition and the search leads to perpetual failure.

It is what we do best here. And we are getting better at what we do.

Everything leads to this conclusion. The fences all have holes. The surge of factories create slums. The wars against drugs somehow manage to lower drug prices and increase drug supplies. The crackdowns on the movement of people make everyone move more often.

There is this huge spread in all the newspapers. A big cocaine cartel out of Bolivia has been taken down. It is a large operation, one with safe houses and centers of business all over this terrain. It is a resident of this place, the edge. For this Ernesto is said to get a fee of a million or more. It is money well earned. When the authorities move to take down the organization, Ernesto is still with the Bolivians. It is close but he makes it. And then he vanishes for a while into a program that is supposed to offer him protection.

The pictures at the exhibition are a problem. We are sitting in a patio watching the sun die and the night come on. Bats appear to hunt in the dusk. The desert slowly cools around the huddled cactus. I am listening to a man who hangs pictures at exhibitions. He is telling me about Ciudad Juarez, about how in the last sixty days teenage gangs have murdered ninety people. He says this killing is the product of turf wars, the result of the collapsing economy. The cheap tabloid weeklies favored by working people in Mexico are rich with photographs of this carnage, of slashed throats, brains blown out, various mutilations. The images, he continues, are incredible in their power. In fact they remind him of the work of Weegee, the fabled New York City photographer of the forties and fifties who roamed murder scenes and whose life's work is now part of the official canon of twentieth-century photography. When I ask why he does not hang these pictures at an exhibition, he says that is not possible because people on this side wish to pretend the other side does not exist. I ask him no more questions.

Or I am in the studio of a graphic artist. She is designing promotional literature for a proposed truck crossing near Ciudad Juarez. The images of this port of entry are beautiful with clean, orderly buildings, with wonderful housing for the human beings who will work in the twin plants, with cheerful factories that produce no smoke or any other visible effluent. The images in her promotional work have a Norman Rockwell quality, though they are done in earth tones and seem to display a lot of stucco surface. She is very enthusiastic about this huge development. When I ask her why she is so taken with the project, she says, well, just examine how nice it looks. I ask her no more questions either.

He is still on the same ground I am on. He comes to town, he does business. Little has changed. He has a large ranch. He continues to do other deals. There is that carpet business. He has toyed from time to time with visiting his boyhood home in Chihuahua. He will wait for the right moment. He will return as a successful man. He has learned the rules of this place and he loves the feel of this place. He is on no goverment commissions, it is true, and he is not mentioned as a role model in any plans I've run across. But this hardly matters. He is here and he is what here is about. He has mastered the jittery quality, he is a pioneer of this new thing.

The writing is on the wall and this time the wall is in Ciudad Juarez. Spray paint outlines a dead body, then comes the time, and finally, the claim—"killed by la migra [U.S. immigration forces]." There are fewer and fewer empty walls these days. Surfaces clutter with growing messages and the messages are increasingly angry. Boxy lettering, crude sketches, a disdain of design, pure anger, a wail catching at the eye without warning, documents erupting overnight, all superseded by newer and more urgent statements, a kind of novel being written by anonymous hands and being read furtively by strangers as they prowl the streets. A new face is coming into view and the authorities describe this face as something that is defacing the public world. A century after the emergence of the penny press and the yellow press and the tabloid, a new publishing revolution comes to the walls and t-shirts and bodies in the edge, a howling screed that says nothing at length and very little with love (hearts with arrows are becoming rare on the walls and boulders and bridge abutments). There is a frenzy of writing life down and all this writing is done at a shout and a run.

I am in southern Chihuahua and the storefront painted black simply says "THE ROAD TO HELL."

Sometimes the handwriting is on an actual piece of paper. I first met Nick in a steakhouse he was managing. He'd gone to work as a boy, leaving school around the fourth or fifth grade. He explained to me that this was normal; the family had so many mouths to feed. As he spoke, he still looked like a boy. A letter comes and I do not need to check the postmark. I know this is a letter from the edge.

You know I had to leave for several reasons. I went to work for a restaurant in Soap Lake, Washington and it was a great experience. Unfortunately, I had to come back to Mexico for Christmas and I couldn't go back. This year I took some time away from people because I had a little emotional reversal. I say it that way because I think what happen is that I was tired of people. So I went working for a concrete company as a watch man in a junk yard they have. Sometimes in a whole day, I didn't see people at all. Then I got to read a lot and little by little I got into the track again to work into something more exciting: The problem was to look for something. I look all over and I saw that in Mexico where you can make money is working in the tourist business or driving an eighteen wheels truck carrying goods from the U.S. to Mexico. I've decided on the last one, driving a truck, so I am now training for it.

You know I had been thinking about writing a book and I still think about it. What I want to write I would have to include some fiction in it, but with a story very realistic and constructive in it. It would include some history from U.S., Mexico and the world. It would be the story of a man who is looking and searching for his own identity. All the stories are similar, aren't they? This one, I have the conviction, it would be different. It would be about domestic politics, overseas politics, human relations, love, money and a dream.

Now I feel like entering the world again—to the race rats. Dreaming doesn't cost at all.

Or I am in a living room and the man is bobbing and weaving as he talks in a jittery way, his words following a rhythm as unpredictable as a jazz guitar at four A.M. in an after-hours club. He is a thin man with a thin mustache and he is brown and blue. His body is drenched in decades of tattoos, all acquired in the various joints that have served as way stations in his career. Naked women, testaments to honor or mother, strange demonic shapes all scroll across his back and chest and arms. He is said to be a killer, a junkie, a dealer, and a pimp. These are trifling matters to him. He is a navigator of the edge. He ticks off the organizations and his problems, a federale owned in one place, a hostile cartel to be wary of in another. He thinks he is dying but at some level he cannot believe in this alleged clinical fact. He has survived too long to believe he can die. He is said to have murdered a half dozen in prison, more on the outside, and now rumor has it he is running wild, crazy with violence because of this black cloud of death hanging over his head. He laughs all the time and has a very winning smile.

He lectures me about methadone—once when he got out of the joint, he was a methadone counselor for a spell—about how terrible it is, how it destroys your bones and that in the interest of sound health it must always be avoided. Heroin, that is what he recommends, heroin will not tinker with your bones. He is very animated as he stresses this point.

Mexico, that too is a word he tosses around. He's just been down arranging a shipment, lining up the new federale chief for payoffs. He advises that it can be crazy down there, that they don't believe in no laws or nothing. He seems shocked by this fact. Once, he rolls on, he got taken down with another guy in Juarez. They were running something or stealing something, that's all a detail now, what matters is the night they spent in jail. Man, he exclaims, it's crazy there. See, he's in this cell with his partner and there's this big Indian guy too and the Indian gets like hostile, you know, and threatens his friend, and what the big guy doesn't know is that his friend has this huge knife hidden under his shirt on his back and so he whips out this blade, man you shoulda seen it, and he goes boom, boom, boom, and man, you could see that blade go in the guy's chest and come out his back three times, and it was beautiful. The big guy went down stone dead. Then them Mexican cops came, took a look and just dragged the body away, like nothing happened you know.

What happened next?

Next? Oh, his partner got killed trying to knock off a jewelry store back across the line.

Leaning against the wall in the living room is a sword cane and it is handed to the man with the tattoos. He caresses it lovingly and then pulls out the blade and exclaims, this is beautiful, man this would feel so good going in, and he starts jabbing at the air and a big smile sweeps across his face.

The tattoos, are the tattoos of the same woman or of different women? He pauses in his jabbing, plunges the sword back into the throat of the cane, rolls up his shirt, and starts ticking off the ladies that ride his body with simmering blue smiles. You can almost see faint hints of memory playing on his face as he rubs their faces with his finger. They say he murdered his first wife when he and she were both teenagers. And then he sent her family the bill for the funeral. No one has ever nailed him for a killing. Luck of the draw. He sits there explaining the snarl of tattoos, all these messages on his body. The writing is everywhere now.

A rainbow floats on the white wall in the alley and below with words and a heart symbol is the message "WE LOVE YOU." Nearby is a dumpster. They found the arms here. The body has never surfaced. The arms came off a teenage girl. For a while the joke circulated that at least we could be confident she did not hitchhike out of town. A crescent moon hovers on the wall surrounded by stars. The walls says, "God bless you," or it says, "Never To Be," or it says, "R.I.P." Sparky says simply, "I Love You." The messages are written over each other, the urgency of a new message casting aside the importance of older messages. "Fly To The Angels. Forever. We Will.

My Daug. . ." So much scribbling under the rainbow in the lonely alley with the dumpster. Sometimes there are candles, bunches of flowers. It is a visitation point for the moment, here, in the edge. A small sign on a post advises that one should not park in this alley. In Juarez on a garage door is a man pointing a huge gun and advising it is dangerous to park in front of that particular garage door. The place is getting tattooed, messages everywhere, shouts inscribed by strange hands, things stated that do not make the newspapers.

A border, well, a border implies a sense of power, of order. An edge states a tension. You do not stand on the border of a volcano. You stand on the edge of a

volcano and wonder how much longer the cauldron will continue sleeping. You stand on the edge of a fault, on the edge of a cliff. Here, everywhere is the edge. The main streets, the alleys, the bodies with blue tattoos. The dumpster in the alley says, "Happy Thanksgiving Wherever You Are." The man fondling the sword cane says, I'm going to get me one of these, man, it would feel so good going in.

It is always a comfort to ignore these facts. Chihuahua is the largest state in Mexico. The region as a whole is ripe with opportunity, with twin plants, growing trade, more and better environmental controls, new commissions working on mutual problems, larger police forces. Bigger plans. Hands across the border. No need to worry. Just look at the lines on the maps.

But underneath the cries of order something new is emerging, something still seeking that word which will be its name. An orphan child of two nations, two ebbing nations, a jittery child given to nervous quick bursts of spray paint. An edge.

I am standing by the road in Chihuahua looking at a small white house with a larger-than-life painting of the Virgin of Guadalupe on its front wall. A lake snores nearby, the waters lie still in the morning light. By the lake some local madman keeps painting huge murals on the boulders. You must walk to view them and then when you do, there is no explanation of their meaning or how they came to be, just the soft lapping of the waters on the lake's edge, and the explosions of color off the rocks. The man lives in the small nearby town and he comes out here and paints these things out of some secret place in his head. He is not finished yet although the scale and trajectory of this project is locked inside his heart. People walk down to the lake and look—I can see scattered beer cans and broken bottles that mark their visits—but this day it is still and quiet.

I became hungry and now I stand by the road near the house with the wall hosting the Virgin and a man squats by a skillet on a small stove and heats up meat for some tacos. He is in his late thirties and lives here. He has worked in Denver, Idaho, and I think, California. Now he is back for a while to be with his family. Then he will go north again and work. I run into these people everywhere—they speak intimately of slaughterhouses in Dodge City, Kansas, of potato fields in Idaho, of the crime festering in west coast cities and how terrible the traffic is in those places. Sometimes the women worry about gangs and the danger to the morals of their children. I once drank with a man who had nineteen brothers and sisters huddled in National City next to San Diego. There is the man on the train who introduced himself by smiling and saying, "I am a wetback." He mowed the lawns for a major research hospital in the states. They always share their techniques for going back and forth, but really these tales are not very exciting to me or to them. There is a perfunctory quality to these journeys. Everything the authorities dwell upon—the barriers, the documents, the plans, quotas, rules—is for these residents of the edge like flies buzzing around one's face, annoying but not a serious matter.

I used to hunt such people with the authorities. We would ride in four-wheel-drive vehicles, leap out and examine tracks in the dust, call over the radio to bring in spotter aircraft, and bust people huddling in bushes with their little plastic jugs of water. It was fun, the hunt and sometimes the chase. We would load them up, take them to headquarters, put them in a holding cell, ask them questions, and then ship them back where they came from. They'd come in all ages and both sexes and they could walk forever. The authorities told me our prey had been born walking and it was something they knew how to do. Once in a while, we'd find bones of those who could not walk so well. I especially liked the tracking, finding the faint impressions, seeing through the efforts to fool us, and then the pursuit, running these aliens to ground. Then one day, for various reasons, I decided to switch sides, to see what it felt like to be hunted. The journey took a long night and brought a lot of pain, but the victory was sweet. After that I increasingly violated the thing called the border, skipping back and forth. Finally, I started removing signs. The signs bothered me. I learned about the obscenity of signs from coyotes. For years I noticed that whenever I seemed to stumble upon a brass survey marker on the earth left by government map makers, the federal marker was buried in coyote scat. So I became a menace to the signs of the authorities. Sensors in the earth also annoyed me. And then I guess I escalated and began to study the techniques of import/export people, navigators who moved tons and tons of materials across the fabled border without a blink and did not pay official tariffs and frankly, kept to very exacting schedules. One day I realized the real borders are things that if you cross you felt alien, felt foreign. And that these points on the earth were not where the authorities had told me. Quite the opposite in fact. What they said was border was actually the very heart of my world, close to the dead center, and that from their made-up line my world radiated outward. I began to shed the notions of nations and take up a sense of place. This sense of place cut through the gibberish of states, of cultures, of rules.

So I wind up standing by a road in what they call Chihuahua, waiting for the meat to heat in a skillet so that a man can sell me a couple of tacos. I feel I am in the same place I came from, I am on home ground. Of course, there are these matters that the experts and authorities keep throwing up at us: different languages, backgrounds, a lot of range in skin colors. And of course the matter of having our documents in perfect order. And if we argue any of these points, they haul out their maps and clobber us with them. No matter. The aroma of the meat heating up is driving me crazy with hunger. The man hunched over his little stove, how carefully he stirs and tends his carne. He and I have more in common than we can fully say at the moment. We are still sweeping away the cobwebs of rules and nationality but we are living the life that ignores their border. We are in a new place and in time we will forge the new language. We are the orphans of the authorities and day by day this fate begins to suit us and day by the day this fate continues to form us.

The man finally hands over the tacos on a paper plate after fussing for a while with his skillet. These hot tacos with various salsas are more real to me and to him than the word *border*. I have lost a grip on things, words like *border*, even words like *Chihuahua*. Colors scream around me—a sky too blue, a Virgin of Guadalupe too brilliant, walls everywhere shamelessly beaming primary colors. I fumble at this sound coming up out of my throat. I lick the jagged piece of lava in my mouth and slowly, ever so slowly to be sure, it gets smoother. I whisper one word to myself and am surprised by the soft sound in the light that throbs toward midday.

June 22, 1894

Along about 11 o'clock that morning we were on a mountain side and decided to eat lunch under a big oak tree which casts an inviting shade for all weary prospectors.

I had a pick and my canteen was attached to the handle by the strap. I laid these down about six feet from where I seated myself to eat. The Mexican had nothing but a small hatchet, such as is usually used by prospectors. After a little while I arose to get a drink, and as I reached for the canteen I saw, not more than six feet away, a big mountain lion creeping along cat-fashion toward me. I seized the handle of the pick and struck the animal as it sprang at me. The lion struck me a glancing blow with one of its fore paws as it passed, and I was knocked headlong into a clump of brush, my face and hands being badly lacerated by coming in hard contact with the limbs.

When I regained my feet the lion was coming toward me again. His hair stood up like a cat's, and his eyes were like balls of fire . . . As he was making ready to spring, the Mexican . . . threw a rock at him, striking him on the head. The lion rolled over several times, and as I picked up a rock to throw at him we were almost paralyzed to see a lioness standing only a few feet further up the hill at our backs . . .

We commenced to back away slowly and at last were off some distance. We ascended the mountainside a short way and got on a shelf rock, where we felt secure. The lion and lioness watched us for at least fifteen minutes....Presently two cubs appeared under the tree and commenced to nurse at their mother's breast.

We lost no time getting away from the locality.

There are of course many details to be worked out. Take an example: Pancho Villa used to live in El Paso and was keen on North American guns and technology. During one brief interlude in the revolution, he ordered the most modern refrigeration units so that he could properly launch his meat markets in Ciudad Chihuahua. On the other hand by the latter part of the revolutionary decade he issued a plan: to destroy any railroad tracks within sixty miles of the Mexican-United States line lest the huge economy to the north swallow his country. This same tension continues to this day.

You will often doubt your own feelings. You will get up in the morning and believe in all the maps, feel the border is rock hard and real, and listen to a president and perhaps for a moment, the voice you hear will not sound like the phantom it is. We all have these moods. I have driven the big roads of Chihuahua, four lanes with shoulders, and it is hard not to believe it is all solid and powerful. The officials help sustain these feelings. The various stamps and forms, the queues at the customs houses, the men with uniforms and semiautomatic pistols riding on their hips—all of these vestments and rituals help maintain the illusion. Behind the various police are the sacred orders of technocrats, all trained up and gelded at the same academies, all very sure of their charts and forecasts, all fingering the same dead birds and studiously ignoring the live eagles flying overhead. These men and women are so certain. In the special institutes they are injected with big syringes full of the hormones of science. They insist that what they say is reality, that there is no way out without them, that everything else is illusion. Repeat after us, they demand, repeat our words and you will be saved, the baby will not die, the wire will hold, the money will flow by artesian pressure, the future will come upon us like the sun at dawn. They have formulas, computers to churn their magic, secret techniques for plumbing the dark heart of the world. All our protests seem feeble, all our ideas sound like complaints. They are the new Bolsheviks. They are certain of their right. The radio is blaring as I listen to the technocrats. One well educated voice is warning me not to cross a line, screaming that such an act is dangerous. I move toward the barbs.

You will run your fingers along the wire of the fence and the barbs will cut, your blood will trickle from your hand, and you will say, yes, yes, this is very real. But this mood cannot be sustained. It is a virtual reality and when the wind picks up the other reality will roar in and bite the skin.

What the eyes see, the heart truly feels. And it sees people moving at will and they are not on television screens. And it hears voices in the street and in the next room and they are not coming off a radio. The handwriting is on the wall, crude and spray painted, but still on the wall. The colors are screaming and shattering the calm of the day. What will happen here in this place is escaping the control of things like nations. Sometimes it seems like a marriage, sometimes more like a collision but still it keeps happening. The only thing that could reverse this trend is unlikely—the return of might and prosperity to the two nations stancing and posing by their creation, this thing they call the border.

The birds do not obey the idea of border. Neither do the plants spreading and invading willy-nilly. The toxic chemicals in the water and the air also scamper about without a thought of borders. I wish to walk to the front of a room, pick up a piece of chalk, and then, in a few quick strokes, sketch this thing being born. But I cannot. I can see it, my heart feels it, but it is still too alive to surrender to the simple outline. It stays hidden—often beneath national identity documents, talk of rising crime, tables about the illegal movement of people. Symptoms disguise its presence from us. Sometimes a photograph captures its elusive presence: a wall shouting colors and hosting a sign announcing Marlboro cigarettes. All these mixtures can be easily dismissed as happenstances and we can recline back into our slumbers, perhaps channel surf in the safe tidy worlds beamed down to us in our lairs.

I lie in a hotel room in Chihuahua, I am locked away in a hotel room in otro lado. I spin through the channels in the television and I am never able to keep the worlds segregated, the flow right before my eyes on the screen. The voices, the images, they talk a babble. They confound order. The set clicks off, the eye goes dark, and silence returns for a moment. It feels safer that way.

But we all know it is not.

Like a lioness with her kittens, we may be puzzled by what is happening, we may be at first mystified by strangers, but in the end we will realize where we are. We will find a word for it. We will suddenly feel a surge of energy, of hormones or power and take the ground as our ground. We will become dangerous, lash out, make animal sounds that will disgust and frighten those who stumble upon us. Perhaps, we will become a quaint clip in their newspapers, a tale told about something dark and bestial at the edge of true order. But we will gradually, inevitably come into ourselves. All this frenzy and jittery feeling and activity will come to something and we will be what it comes too. The clipping will grow yellow with age and be filed and almost forgotten. The kittens will grow and live and breed and probe ever more deeply into their ground. They will flourish beneath the notice of most, they will persist, and they will still be there when the clip crumbles into dust. You think this is a fantasy?

So did some men in the 1890s who hailed from a world of progress and manifest destiny and certainty.

I know, I know, you want something a little classier, a bit more substantial. Something solid, like the Greek front of an old time bank, perhaps, or the thundering might of a *palacio municipio.* So do I. But it is not in the cards right now. Azatlan? That would be nice and comforting. Gran Chichimeca? That also has a ring. We have consumed and destroyed the cheap rhetoric of *twin plants, hands across the border, multi-culturalism, la raza, Proposition 187,* and that old chestnut, *sovereignty.* These words imply a security we surrendered by the very act of coming to this place. All the fine words have an allure, I admit. But they are finished. And we are not. We are becoming. We are going toward something. But we are not there yet, not nearly there. We are an unfinished thing and we must go with what we now are. We must not be seduced by the easy answers of the planners and economists and diplomats or politicians. We will have to go with what we have at the moment.

Sometimes, to be frank, I think that when we will know and I will know, at that moment, this future will come as a woman. Perhaps, this is because I am a man. For a year, I hid near this fabled border in an abandoned ranch house and each morning I rose and looked at a huge scar let by earlier immigrants into this ground, creatures called *vacas,* cattle. Nothing had grown on this wound for a century, nothing. The soil was gone, just rock remained. I was living in the hills and each night caravans of drug laden horses paced by and moved softly under a faint moon toward markets. This I paid little heed to. But the wound caught my eye and then down the hills I found the place where the scant waters of the hard ground came to rest in a *cienaga,* a bog. That is where I saw the thing as the form of a woman. She rose up from the stagnant waters, her hair long and coarse, her hips girdled with a skirt of lichen. In her nose was not a bone but the spine off an agave. Her eyes were smeared dark from the char of ten thousand years of fires. A necklace of skulls rode around her neck and I did not see this as morbid. I saw this as real and local like the candies munched here and there on the day of the dead. Her breasts were hidden by bandoleers and her face wore a gypsy smile, La Guitana. A raven rested on her shoulder and two eagles flapped after her wherever she went. A coyote followed her like a dog and the purse hanging off one shoulder and riding against a hip had the long hairs of the wolf. She was barefoot but earrings of gold and silver dangled and gave off bell-like tones as she moved. Her skin was rich with color, reds, blues, whites, greens gleaming from a field of brown. The eyes were clear and alert but still at ease. She carried no passport and spoke softly and was well mannered. She seemed at ease. Once I saw her visit the falcon's nest on the cliff face and her steps never faltered. Her moves on the rock face were sure and fluid.

I would walk with her through the deserts and mountains and cross the hills dotted with oak. Sometimes we rested under the pines of the high ground, choppers whomping overhead, spotter aircraft just barely cresting a hill and then spilling down the slopes to hunt. I would leap and fling the finger at them and shout obscenities but she would never ever look up at such moments. Her eyes were on the ground and I felt blind. She keep finding everything, seeing everything, and I followed her as a child trailing after a teacher. When she smiled her teeth were white and even. The animals did not fear her and, when hungry, she roasted them on spits. At night bats fluttered around her face and brushed her skin with their light wings. She never went to town. I cannot remember a word she said. I am not even sure of the language. Once we came upon a crime scene and she chewed through the tape of the police barrier. I saw her with my own eyes leave jugs of water by hot trails for the travelers who might come. I awoke at midnight and heard her singing the song of the humped-backed whale. Once in the flush of an afternoon's sun she strummed a guitar and sang "Adelita." She always picked the best buds and dried them well. We bedded down in sleeping circles and she knew all the stars. Her fingers left no prints no matter how carefully I dusted. I can still remember her dancing with a deer head atop her mane of black hair while flailing at an electric guitar. She burned all official vehicles, the black columns of smoke in her wake violating the sky. I could never detect her favorite color. But everything around her was very bright and primary. Her body drenched in various paints, I followed her into a country not yet named.

The jagged piece of lava in my mouth cuts my tongue and I bleed. Yet the stone slowly smoothes.

The camera clicks, we stare at the transparency on the light table. We know that everything we need to know is in the image. We merely have to face it.

Treason becomes a slippery concept, one harder and harder to grasp. Just as breaking the law seems to weigh less and less each day. Loyalty draws nearer. I can feel the breath of loyalty on my face.

There's a dance going on. You can hear the guitar, the drum, the man with the harp in his mouth, the women singing, even a tuba, two tubas for that matter, and a wall of horns now blasting, now wailing, now riding desert winds, now coursing mountain canyons. The dance should be very fashionable here on the edge, should be at the very height of fashion: it is the dance, well, we shall call it the dance of empowerment. And this dance does not give power to you but recognizes the power in you. It is scored by neglect, financed by repression and the solid back beat comes from contempt. They, the mythical *they* of governments and rules, think we are less than nothing, a mere appendage to this real thing which is themselves, the governments and their nations. We are the back room, the back-street girl as it were, the border. We are basically nothing to them but a place to store their police and to worship their imaginary lines on the map.

Whenever I mention this dance to others—this frenzy that I feel growing and bopping to the ebbing powers of the governments and the growing powers of ourselves—well, when I mention the steps and sly moves of the dance, I'm met with disbelief or denial. I'm told about the treaties, the satellites, the technologies, the new world global village, the chains of Internet, the . . . the objections never seem to end. I feel at these moments that I'm back in school and the teacher pulls the map down from its curled form—snap!—and stabs at it with a pointer—bam!—and shouts: There is the border! There are the state boundaries! There are the radar blimps! There are the tactical air commands! There are the customs houses! There are the police stations! There, dammit, there! And it always reminds me of sitting through sex education in high school—the teacher simply does not sing a song I can dance to. I can feel this edge, see it flowing around me, spot it in new trucks, old huts, our own faces.

That is where this thing of empowerment comes in. They don't give power to us, they are simply losing it, losing power, and so the juice, the fire, the electricity of possibility rain down upon us, rock our flesh, crack our bones and nail our minds to the place, the edge. The authorities are desperate you see, they've used up their bandoleers—*Socialism, Communism, the New Deal, the Party of the Institutional Revolution*—

and they're down to their last bullet, one they call amongst themselves *capitalism*, and one they tell us is *free trade*. I see them, the presidents on screens at the local bar, and their images are beamed down from their nefarious satellites and eaten by big discs and then fed into the huge screen floating at one end of the room. These presidents look like robots and talk like robots and they carry their GATTs and fondle their NAFTAs and beam with the expectations of what life will soon be like for all of us global villagers. They say they have freed money from the lines on the map and are freeing goods from the lines on the map and, by this magic, they will trap people within the lines on the map. Sometimes I cannot tell the presidents apart unless the camera catches a glimpse of the flags they always keep near them like talismans. For a while, I was sure they were witches because they kept chanting the same words over and over. But then I gave up this notion. Witches' words have power. I live in a place where witches still operate, I've seen them with my own eyes. They do not look like these presidents or behave like them either. The presidents are not people of the edge, a fact inscribed on their smooth faces.

They are prisoners of these big notions, *global economies* and *nations*. We to a man, woman, and child are pretty much the rejects of these notions. We are the ones nobody wants. We're like the dead whales that bob in the sea by our shores, the ones killed mysteriously by something natural or unnatural, the huge leviathans rotting on the beaches and beneath the concern of the authorities. We are like the dead hulks of haciendas in Chihuahua, there but not really recognized as *there*. And if recognized from time to time in quaint historical publications, they are swiftly dismissed again lest the meaning of their deaths and huge mud bones stab into the consciousness of the planners and rulers.

That is why the dancing is increasingly possible, why the music is picking up.

A friend comes out from New York City and she is at the place I'm staying about four miles from the fetish zone, the line they say separates the United States from Mexico. I ask her, "How do you like it here?" She says, "I think I'm in a foreign country." I say nothing then, the rock in my mouth was still too rough, still required more smoothing by my tongue. So I did not say the word out loud, did not even whisper to myself . . . Edge.

The presidents have no bullets left, only they do not realize it yet. But we know. It is the reality jerking our limbs, moving our feet, lifting us from our slumbers, and causing us to dance.

I have these thoughts, overwhelming stories that storm my mind and ride me like visions or nightmares. In this—what should I call it?—story that takes over my mind, it is the year 1929 and the floor is falling and there are no railings to grasp as the dark, cold air rushes up and storms around my face. I look at my hands. The skin is red, the fingers are crabbed and shrunken. I open the icebox and the shelves are bare except for a rancid piece of salt pork wrapped in greasy wax paper. Out on the back porch the milkman has left me a quart I can't afford. The cream has frozen and oozed out the top. I sold the radio last week and now all my hopes lie in a rent party. I think of killing myself, I really do. My dress slacks have a gravy stain, my suit coat is shiny, my left shoe has a whole in the sole. So I think about death all the time. It seems the easiest thing. But I lack the necessary energy. I don't own a gun and now I can't afford one. I look out the window from my third floor walkup and feel the pull of the street down below. But even climbing out on the ledge and then pitching forward requires more will than I now possess. Something has been done to me and I am not sure what it is or who has done it. I just know it has been done. I have expectations that are not being met—yes, that is it, they are not being met. Promises were made, damn it, and I have a right to expect those promises to be fulfilled. I am a failure but this cannot be helped. It is not my fault. At least I think it is not my fault. Then again I am not so sure at times. I am afraid. Of everything.

Still, I think of opening the window and falling, falling like a leaf on a warm day in Indian summer. Black Tuesday of 1929 has let the air out of the big balloon I know as Wall Street. Out beyond the safe concrete, the land has been starving the people for years. Every hog is worth too little, every cow is a drain, every field is an indictment of personal worth, and the granaries are full but have no value. Of course, there is Babe Ruth and Lindy has made it. But nothing can stop these waves of fear rolling through the flesh, nothing can prevent the sweat on the brow on a winter day. The women are still there but we do not go to them. The men are still there but they no longer can function and pleasure us.

Christopher Morley, a writer, has been invited to the White House for a visit with President Herbert Hoover. Outside the building no one is certain what to believe because all the beliefs are falling down and there seems to be no bottom. It is tidy, this collapse coming at the very end of a decade. This fact rings some alarm deep within us. We are keen for the round finality of numbers—a Biblical thing?—no one is certain. But we sense an era, an age, an epoch, is finishing and a future is unfolding that we cannot make out and clearly cannot face. We are beginning to blame—the plutocrats, unfeeling politicians, international bankers. Soon we will discover Jews, Communists, labor agitators, blacks. Our list will grow and grow. Still, we have the Babe and we trust him. In fact we pay him more than the President but then as the Babe explains, he's had a better year. He is our dream, a man of action. He drinks all night and takes a cab to the stadiums and still is able to perform as the Sultan of Swat. He takes a woman to his hotel room and when he is ready to go to work in the morning, his roommate asks him how he made out the night before. The Babe says, count the cigar butts in the ashtray. His roommate counts seven stubs smoked down to the very end. The Babe does not falter. There is no fear in his fat smooth face.

But, as the Big Bambino has pointed out, President Hoover has not had a good year. He knows it but he does not understand why. Unlike you and I, though, the president is not . . . well, he is not afraid. He understands the world, possibly the universe, and all that needs to be done right now is a little adjustment. He asks the nation's businessmen not to cut wages so that people will spend and then factories will reopen and machines will once again sing. He tells the capital's Gridiron Club that "the most dangerous animal in the United States is the man with an emotion and a desire to pass a new law." He is an engineer by training and for engineers every problem has a solution and every solution is by the book and by the numbers. This habit of thought precludes fear. Still, he senses something is loose in the land and this nameless, formless, yet hydra-headed thing is dangerous to him and to what he represents because this thing is emotional and angry and afraid. It is an obscene thing to the president because it is to him something irrational.

Morley quite naturally wonders why in the middle of a national crisis he has been summoned to the White House. Hoover is not a man to waste time on small talk. He explains,

> What this country needs is a great poem. Something to lift people out
> of fear and selfishness. Every once in a while someone catches words out
> of the air and gives a nation an inspiration . . . . I'd like to see something
> simple enough for a child to spout in school on Fridays. I keep looking for
> it but I don't see it . . . . Let me know if you find any great poems lying
> around.

That is where the dream or story ends, always, with the search for the great poem, the trick of words that will lift us up, solve all the problems, and make the crooked way straight. I never found the poem, nor did Hoover for that matter. He just kept on rattling off technocratic madness until the end of his days. He was a foreshadower, I suspect, of the presidents that flutter on the big screen in my local cantina. Right now, I'm sure they'd like a nifty poem. I'm certain they are tired of doing everything by the numbers. But they haven't got a prayer. You see, they live in the wrong place. They don't know the edge. But we do. It is all we know lately. And it is more intrusive, harder to deny. The blade of the knife, certain, definite, yet fluid, what with the blood spewing forth from this path in the flesh.

The house is brick and it seems no one lives there. The rooms lack furniture though they do have weights and benches and nautilus machines for working out. It sits in the desert on the edge of a city. Then, one day, there will be a dozen or two dozen young men lounging about the place. The young men are in fine shape and very muscular and for a day or two they will be there lifting weights and working out. Suddenly they will vanish and no one will be around the house for a week or two or three. It goes on like that, a cycle with its own private and natural rhythm. The young men look capable of say toting a hundred pound load hour after hour over a mountain or across a very hot desert. They look like they could reach their destination, drop their loads and turn around and go back for yet another load. The house is here in the edge. Which side of their border it sits on is not a serious matter since it could and is on both sides.

    Then there is this man who meets a boy. The kid drops into his store each day and just hangs out. The man does not mind. The boy is very quick and he admires this trait. The boy grows older and is a young man. He comes to the storeowner with a proposition: would he drive a van each weekend for an hour or two. The man says yes. For a year or two he drives a van full of men and drops them off and then they walk away with backpacks. A day later, he returns and picks up the men, just the men, nothing else. For this work he receives one thousand dollars a week. Every week. That is all the shopkeeper does. He never sees anything. He never does anything but drive a van load of men. He does this for several years and never asks any questions. He still likes the quickness of the boy who hung around his shop.

Once in Chihuahua, the truck dipped down into a little valley where a stream leaving the sierra settled into its course and then reached the edge of the great desert waiting to swallow it. Down in this little valley, there were many trees. One building had a huge tree flowering out of its roof and looked like the shelter of some hobbit. The calles of the small town were narrow, the walls very brilliant with colors. Then the truck turned on the sidestreets and they became lanes of dirt winding their way through trees that lined the route. The lots were small here, an acre or less, and often they were marked by mud walls. Everything in this bottom was cool and green and the houses were small and the people poor. Election declarations were painted everywhere as the government tried to claim possession of the clucking chickens and little houses and trees and tiny fields that passed before my eyes. People would look up, birds screamed in the trees above, dogs slept in the lanes and moved slowly and sullenly. A big vote on a nation was coming in a few days but here in this forgotten pocket I could not connect the ground with the ballot. I could not even believe in the ballot. I do not think I was alone in this inability.

Oh, yes. About the mountain lions? The authorities have never been able to kill them off. About the people crossing the wire marking the imaginary line on the sacred map? The authorities have never been able to stop them—delay them, but not stop them. About the drugs? They move faster and easier than the money.

The colors are getting louder. Soon I suspect they'll drown out the police sirens. The power is right there, in the air—breathe it. In that tumbler on the table, drink it. In your heart, feel it.

Don't call home.

You're already there.

Edge.

It's the only game left in town.

Whales bobbing on the waves, whales rotting on the beaches. Then there are the squadrons of dolphins riding dead in the waters. It becomes a problem. So naturally the nations throw in their agents and studies are done. There are these laboratories,

Why the Writing Stops

these computers. We are not helpless. We can give you the answers you want. It all happened on this sea some call the Sea of Cortez. Ah, you say, what does this have to do with Chihuahua? What, for that matter, does it have to do with Estados Unidos? That is a very good question—set up the seminar, request the scholarly papers and, by all means, have maps, satellite imagery, and computer data analysis.

Do not worry, the preliminary reports are in. The tissue samples, El Señor, indicate a very high level of mercury. Ah, thank God, now we understand. However, there is a slight problem: the reported mercury levels in the tissues of the dead sea beasts are below the normal rate for healthy and living sea beasts. And here, alas, we have hundreds and hundreds of them dead on the waters and dead on the beaches. Get those water samples again, we'll run again through the machines, we'll sort this right out. But the further lab reports seem inconclusive. Nature, as we all know, can leave us with mysteries.

There was a ship and the ship was loaded. It headed north into the upper Gulf, the Sea of Cortez, toward that headland which almost brushes against the skin of their border. The authorities appear on the horizon and they pursue. The weight must be lessened—Aye! Aye, mi Capitan!—and paquettes of cocaine are thrown over the side. There are killings also; at least two of the authorities are said to die, but who will ever truly know? The lab reports are notoriously very weak in these matters. The

Dive, I tell you, dive goddammit.

Huge rotting masses of flesh, carrion feeders clustered around but do not worry—the satellites refuse to see us.

data base grows very weak at this point. We have, it is true, this alleged ship full of cocaine, so full the value is rumored to be $15 billion, but let us be honest, a billion is not what it used to be, amigo. The only constant is the bite of the salt air and the screaming of those gulls.

The men tossing the plastic bags over the side, those men I see every morning I lift a sharp edge and shave my face. They are men with women and children, men who wish to live and drink and eat and love. Men who eagerly throw bags of pure cocaine over the side so that this ship may move yet more swiftly and escape. Escape what, you ask? A very fine question. They wish to escape other men with uniforms who desire to possess a ship with $15 billion worth of cocaine in its holds. Forget science, forget political science—we are in another country now, Transactional Analysis. Welcome to the edge.

I'm afraid only part of the conclusion can now be provided. You see, the film itself is being re-edited. You must understand the preview audiences were very disappointed in the director's cut. So we must deal with the available footage. We have—Camera! Rolling!—a ship full of coke, the authorities, bless their souls, in pursuit, men dying, and these white-dream powders going over the side—full steam ahead! After that, on some levels we know nothing. The whole scene vanishes from the our screen. I'll give you tidbits. Whispered words in the ports. Bags washing up on beaches. Bags seen bobbing on the waters. And, I'm sorry, these huge hulks, dead whales to be exact. Then there is the matter of the hundreds of dead dolphins. Sea birds also, but we do not have time for trifles. Ah, I'll save you time—it is a mystery. All we know is that if you can read this page, your breathing is, well, automatic. You do not have to will or think it. But for whales and dolphins, breathing is a deliberate matter. And, it seems cocaine—imagine, amigo, sucking down a line with a straw the size of a telephone pole—is conscious and the beloved white powder breaks this link in your consciousness and you cannot will your breath and you stop breathing and then, you die. That is the story making the rounds at the moment.

I wish to repeat myself. Please indulge me.

A dead whale bobs on the waters of the desert sea, hundreds of dolphins rot on the beaches, the experts scamper to decide what caused this dying, and the nations slowly pivot their attention from the concerns of distant capitals and, for a few seconds, consider who is to blame and is the cause, natural or unnatural, and is the cause, Mexican or American, and is . . . and then they forget about it, as they always do because it all happens on ground that burns and heaves beyond the limits of their attention. A place on a map but surely not within the throb of their national lives. Gulls scream overhead, faxes purr out of machines, the vast bureaucracies of order lumber on and still the whales bob in the sea, an enormous mass of dead flesh too small to sustain the attention of the creatures sitting at desks and staring into the dead eyes of computers. I have lived like the whale in a world beneath notice.

What we need are more reports to be sure. But, I must tell you that does not happen here, not here on the edge. We get dead whales bobbing in the waters, we get maps. Very good maps I must say. And the satellite imagery is dazzling. But the whales, hell, they had a hell of a rush. Best shit they ever snorted. You shoulda been there.

Look, there was this dude in the nineteenth century and he wrote this sentence on a piece of paper. The sentence read, "We make our decisions, and then our decisions turn around and make us."

The whales are diving; but do not worry; no one will notice. Relax, you are off the map. The dolphins, well, there are lots of them to kill. People moving through those wires, drugs moving through this rumored border, money crackling in the air above our heads—while the whales die, hold your breath Moby!

Whales sucking deep, taking a big snort, the muscles pause, then suddenly cannot move. That choking feeling, white powder in the water. The dive begins.

Slipping through the wire, walking the sand of the wash, men, women, children, bodies bent, feet hurrying while the satellites spin overhead officiating over the official order.

Dolphins rotting on beaches, hundreds of dolphins, and finally there truly is a line, that big white line that strangled them to death.

I am a dead whale, I am a gray hawk moving north and south at will, I am footprints in the sand of the arroyo, I am the caravan bringing drugs through the wire, I am free of the state. I am off the map.

Let's do a review, tie it all up in a tidy bundle. Where to begin? Oh, yeah, we're going to grow the economies. Capital can move, goods can move, people stay put. It is organized, we have treaties, all crisp and clear on paper, all cement and guns and stamps and sensors at a place called the border. Adjustments will be made, corn tariffs lowered here, currency exchange rates shored up there, a pooling of data on illicit drug activities. Given time, the standards of living increase, everyone feasts at the new industrial order, the present is secured so that it has a future, the wealth of nations booms, the rational controls the flesh. This is a new world, one we are told is postmodern, or postcolonial, truly it must be post-Cold War. It is simply too hot here for a cold war to be possible. And history has ended, thank God, since we all recall from our schooling what a damn nuisance that history was. The dead animals rolling in the waves certify the new order. They never really existed, they never really died, and if they did really exist and did really die, well, it was the red tide or mercury or an oil spill. The lab reports are on the way or they are already here and no matter. It is solved. True, there will be adjustments, a steel wall here on the border, new search roads bladed there, improved customs houses, special permits, also. Every question that is raised about this new order or about this border is dismissed as a detail, a little problem to be easily solved as we sketch the big picture. There are at least two worlds that I know of. One that believes it can all be directed from the top. The other one, the one swarming around me, the one swarming within me, lives at the bottom and pays little or no attention to the directives from the top. Or I am an official. There has been a large sea mammal die-off in this particular sector of the Sea of Cortez. The appropriate agencies are involved, I assure you. We are examining tissue, samples were taken from vital organs. A full report is at hand. Experts from both nations are conferring. The incident is regrettable but manageable. Any procedural errors will be corrected in the future guidelines. Process can control product. Data bases are self-rectifying. Systems are in order. Further developments will be posted in your E-mail.

Pick your world or just wait: a world will pick you. You can be post- something-or-other. Or you can be the beginning.

At the moment, we are apparently trapped in virtual reality. This cyberspace flings numbers at us. It tells us various police groups have caught huge numbers of illegal human beings. It says that the economies are perking right along or that any problems are statistical perturbations and will soon be ironed out. In this vitural reality low wages, unemployment, murder, narcotics traffic, mass migrations of the poor, depleted treasuries, worthless bonds, collapsing currencies, and giant loans to legendary deadbeats can all be massaged, made logical, wholesome, and nutritious. Watch the screen, boot up the program, dawdle with the mouse, crunch some numbers, bake a few pie charts and suddenly you can believe in the border and in order and in smooth sailing. Banks going under? No, simply a matter of restructuring. Wages falling through the floor? Hardly, great new career opportunities, simply an opening for job retraining. There is nothing now—starvation, desperation, murder, pollution, pain, flight, a needle in the arm, and relief flooding the vein—there is nothing now, I tell you, that we cannot handle with a spreadsheet. And as we go into this new full lotus, there is nothing the spreadsheet cannot massage and smooth and make okay. Just look at the screen and stop your crying. It must have been very much like this at the court of Louis the Sixteenth. Or perhaps in the palace of Czar Nicholas as Rasputin purred in the ear of the Czarina. No doubt the last meetings of the ruling group under Mikhail Gorbachev had the same wonderful sense of assurance as this cyberspace. Somewhere at this moment a frivolous and crazed Queen is saying, "Let them eat software." So stay glued to the screen, wallow in the interactive features, take a ride on the information highway. Perhaps, we simply should enjoy it while we can. They tell us the chips are getting faster and faster, the screens improving constantly, the sound systems roaring against our hungry ears. Hitler in his bunker moving dead across a meaningless map has nothing on us with our voyages through cyberspace. Virtual reality is pretty good. Until the real world shows up.

We live in a war and this war is an effort to stop the future. Everyone now talks about the past, about restoring something that once was good and that once worked. Such talk hasn't got a prayer but this fact seems to still no one's tongue. There is talk, for example, of restoring a dead religion called Free Trade. Once this was the theology of the British Empire and, like most religions, it was good for Sunday morning and put in a closet for the rest of the week. Or there is talk of some kind of populism, some forty acres and a mule, or say forty hectares and a burro, where we all become freeholders, live in sensible semirural accomodations and hammer out material for building the information highway. Oh, Lord, we're going to infrastructure ourselves to death, network until we're more tied up than Promethus, and erase all the color lines with lots of moola that makes the pigment of skin unimportant next to the color of our money.

I remember years ago sitting in a clean room full of computers with satellite link-ups and scurrying helpers who tended the electronic altars. As I watched, a man plied the international waters of exchanges in Singapore or Chicago or New York or London or Zurich or God knows where. I was frankly baffled by the action and when I admitted this, I was told of a new world and if I did not get with the program I would go under and my nation would go under and other people would take over my little world. I got a lecture on Third World debt and what a bargain it was. I got a lecture on debt and what a wonder it was. Mainly, I got a glimpse into a world I had been unable to imagine, a world where money recognized no frontiers and people were supposed to recognize and obey the lines of all borders. My instructor was an expert and like many men ahead of his time, he now sits in a cell and makes big Xs on a calender waiting for the years to roll by and bring him his release date. I was dazzled by his new world view and did not believe a word of it. I thought: what about the growing populations, what about the growing numbers of poor people, what about the sagging earth under this wonderful clean room full of machines, what about pursuing a course of action that made dollars but made no sense? Also, I wondered why does everyone in this new world he described, this world of satellites and computers and global this and that, this world of rules and order and cybernetic fury, why do they all buy a horse as soon as they get some money? Why is everyone looking backward when they claim they're looking forward? Why this war against the future? He brushed aside each and every one of my caveats. He said look at the numbers.

The tally of the authorities for one small slice of their border is: a bag of 25,000 illegal human beings. The whales are largely on the beach, their blubber rotting in the sun, carrion birds tearing at the meat. Big plastic bags are washing up also. More troops and equipment are being deployed. Computers are projecting, fax machines purr in the offices. And footprints continue to appear in the arroyos.

Colors, my God, I can't forget the colors. They are in my face and I love them. The scent also, the thing is a paste being smeared against my flesh. Maps? I'm afraid they are useless at the moment. On the maps, we don't exist. On the maps, nothing you have read has ever happened.

That is life in the edge.

But we will be back.

In the midnight hour.

Listen for bells. They will be proceeded by guitars and possibly our drunken voices will rise in the dark, happy drunken voices. We will sing corridos, tales of valor and sorrow. Women will smile, children will be present. We will be out in the cool of the night under the trees. Over there, under the trees. Watch out, we are breeching. Singing.

The songs will cross all known borders.

But they will have an edge.

Believe it, *compañero*.

Canst thou draw out the leviathan with an hook? or his tongue with a cord

   which thou lettest down?

Canst thou put an hook into his nose? or bore his jaw through with a thorn?

What Someone Else Wrote

Will he make many supplications unto thee? will he speak soft words unto you?

Will he make a covenant with thee? will thou take him for a servant for ever?

Wilt thou play with him as with a bird? or wilt thou bind him for the maidens?

Shall the companions make a banquet of him? shall they part him among the

   merchants?

Canst thou fill his skin with barbed irons? or his head with fish spears?

Lay thine hand upon him, remember the battle, do no more.

. . . . None is so fierce that dare stir him up . . . .

Job, 41: 1-10.

plates

1. Early Morning, Cuauhtémoc

2. Doorway, Hidalgo del Parral

3. *Ruins, Hidalgo del Parral*

4. *Abandoned Hacienda near Santa Barbara*

5. *La Pintura Ideal, Hidalgo del Parral*

6. *Super de Pinturas, Ciudad Juarez*

7. Cemetery, Ciudad Juarez

8. *The Gulp of Mexico, Ciudad Juarez*

9. Near Anahuac

10. *Doorways, Aquiles Serdán*

11. Spam, Delicias

12. Marilyn in Ciudad Juarez

13. Street Corner, Santa Barbara

14. *Near the Rio Grande, Ciudad Juarez*

15. Quinta Carolina and Wolf, Ciudad Chihuahua

16. *Mine and Cemetery, San Francisco del Oro*

17. Baseball Field and Camelot, Nuevo Casas Grandes

18. Mansion, Ciudad Chihuahua

19. *Futurama, Cuauhtémoc*

20. *San Francisco del Oro*

21. Zapata, Ciudad Juarez

22. *Hands above the Border, Ciudad Juarez*

23. Brigada por la Paz, Ciudad Juarez

24. Abandoned German Club, Ciudad Juarez

25. *Graffiti, Hidalgo del Parral*

26. *Video Londres, Cuidad Chihuahua*

27. Scarecrow in Santa Barbara

28. *Dino Burger, Delicias*

29. ¡Cuidado! Ciudad Juarez

30. Door, Ciudad Chihuahua

31. Storefronts, Ciudad Camargo

32. *Batman and Friends, Anahuac*

33. Quonset Hut, Hidalgo del Parral

34. Hollywood Club, Ciudad Juarez

35. Pintore, Ciudad Juarez

36. Red Door, Hidalgo del Parral

37. *Video Flash, Cuauhtémoc*

38. Zapatorama, Cuauhtémoc

39. Hidalgo del Parral

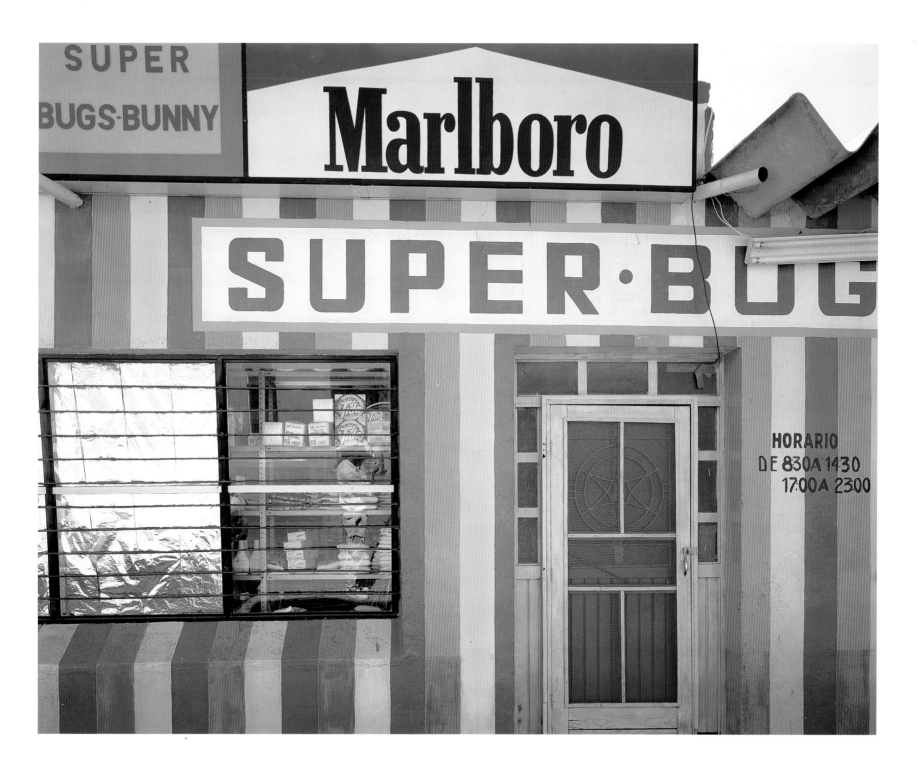

40. *Super Bugs (Self-Portrait), Ciudad Camargo*

Chihuahua: Pictures from the Edge

Typeset in Stone Serif and Stone Sans
with Guts display using Quark Xpress
3.31 for Windows
Text film output by Business Graphics,
Albuquerque, New Mexico
Color separations by C&C Offset Printing
Co., Ltd., from 8 x 10 transparencies
Printed and bound by
C&C Offset Printing Co., Ltd.
Printed in Hong Kong
Designed by Kristina Kachele